Supercharge
Your Notary Business With

LinkedIn®

How Mobile Notaries & Loan Signing Agents
Build Their Brand, Get Known, and Connect
With Their Dream Clients

BILL SOROKA
&
SANDRA LONG

Print ISBN: 978-1-7341833-1-3

eBook ISBN: 978-1-7341833-2-0

GET YOUR FREE BONUS MATERIAL ON THE
SUPERCHARGE YOUR NOTARY BUSINESS WITH
LINKEDIN READER RESOURCE PAGE!

GET FREE ACCESS AT
www.NotaryCoach.com/linkedin

TABLE OF CONTENTS

FOREWORD FROM LAURA BIEWER

I've been collaborating with Bill Soroka now for several years through his Notary Coach brand, and I've been tracking his relationship with Sandra Long, the author of *LinkedIn For Personal Branding: The Ultimate Guide,* as they have consistently nudged us notaries into the LinkedIn arena.

It's a good thing they are consistent and persistent, because I, like so many other notaries I know, have been resistant. It's not that I didn't know that LinkedIn could be a powerful tool, but to me, it just felt like something else that I'd have to manage every day, and that made it easier to bump lower on my priority list each morning.

But, as many of Bill's ideas tend to do, this concept of LinkedIn being able to supercharge my notary and my coaching business really began to simmer and percolate.

I still have plenty to learn and implement myself, and I always will. I think that's one of the things in common that Bill, Sandra, and I share—we will always keep learning and growing—and I encourage you to adopt the same philosophy for your own life and business.

I started with the absolute bare minimum LinkedIn profile, unsure that anyone would even look at it. Slowly, over the years watching various webinars with Sandra and Bill and after reading Sandra's first book, I slowly dabbled and made some changes to my profile.

But this book, *Supercharge Your Notary Business With LinkedIn,* has taken it to a whole new level. I realized that I was missing out on connections, introductions, and potential business relationships. I decided to read it with my LinkedIn account open and ready for additional editing! It was easy as there were directions and examples all along the way.

LinkedIn isn't about building a resume; it's about building relationships. And, like any relationship, first impressions are *everything.* Your LinkedIn profile, combined with the content you provide, the way you interact with your audience, and the messages you send and receive, paint a picture about who

1

you are and what you value. *This* is how your dream clients make the decisions about whether to work with you.

This resource that Sandra and Bill have created is a roadmap to exactly how *any* mobile notary and loan signing agent can feel proud about their business presence online, attract more of the *exact* clients they want, and build the lifestyle they've always dreamed of.

Differentiate yourself from 99% of other notaries and implement what you learn from this book immediately. Every client you could ever dream of is already on LinkedIn. All you have to do is find them and show them the best of what you have to offer. If you want to grow your business by making connections that lead to introductions, collaborations, and relationships that move your business forward as well as give you the opportunity to support those you meet along the way, then this book will make it happen!

See you on LinkedIn!

> —Laura Biewer, Co-host of Tuesday Notary Titans (TNT),
> Founder and Organizer of Notary Symposium,
> Creator of Laura Biewer Presents Replay Library,
> and Owner of "At your Service Mobile Notary"

WHAT PEOPLE ARE SAYING ABOUT
SUPERCHARGE YOUR NOTARY BUSINESS WITH LINKEDIN

John M. Holder, Attorney at Holder and Lykins, P.S.C. | Founder/CEO of KentuckyNotary.net | Kentucky Remote Online Notary

When my ten-dollar notary commission started out-earning my expensive law degree, I was pleasantly surprised. And then my business kept growing. It's now to the point where I'm finding and training local and national notaries to help me fulfill requests. I'm extremely grateful and forever indebted to Bill Soroka and Sandra Long as they've played a huge role in my success. By following their expert advice, I've been able to achieve goals I never thought were possible. When remote online notarization became legal in Kentucky, it was Bill who encouraged me to consider expanding my services beyond the boundaries of my state and nation even–it was time to market to the whole world! Turns out, there's no better way to do that than to heed Sandra Long's guidance when it comes to the LinkedIn platform. It's one thing to connect with people in your community, but by implementing the strategies and techniques detailed in this book, the world is your oyster! Dog-eared pages, notes in the margins, highlighted text on every other page–this is the sign of a well-read book and that's exactly what my manuscript copy of LinkedIn for Notaries looks like. Take the actionable tips and techniques laid out in the following pages and add your personality to them. You'll soon discover that you've elevated your notary/signing agent business to the next level.

Samantha N. Smith, ShelistenS Notary & Business Services

No snake oil sales here. No magic beans, no pot of gold at the end of the rainbow, or little man behind the curtain with a megaphone complete with smoke and mirrors. Bill Soroka, THE Notary Coach, is THE real thing, and he's done it again. *Supercharge Your Notary Business With LinkedIn* is another instruction manual that should be in every notary's arsenal. Bill genuinely connects with experts in the field to provide solid and strategic steps that any notary can follow to positively impact their business. This collaboration with Sandra Long illustrates the power of LinkedIn and how notaries can plugin to this rich resource. The steps and tips provided were immediately applicable and provided real results. I especially liked how specific the steps were. No vague and muddy instructions. Most importantly, everything was laid out with such transparency it's obvious that both Bill and Sandra want to see all notaries succeed. Thank you both for your willingness to impart into the notary community.

Zion Brock, Co-founder of the Get Known Strategy & Founder of The Triple Threat Artist

As one of the power tips in this book states, "As soon as your name is mentioned or referred (in business), expect people to view your LinkedIn profile for further validation."

We all know this to be true . . . I've done this countless times myself when getting ready to hire someone or use their services. And yet so few of us ever really do anything about making this "LinkedIn" thing work to our advantage.

The days of relying on a pocketful of business cards and paper resumes are over. Now, professionals in every industry are expected to have a quality LinkedIn profile. And this couldn't be more true for notaries. Our LinkedIn profile is our digital resume and has become the new normal for how people trust and see you.

The guidance in this book will not only walk you through creating and tailoring your LinkedIn profile through easy step-by-step methods, but will also train you on how to strategize the human connection leveraged by LinkedIn tools to find and create more clients organically.

Bill and Sandra lay out an easy and fun way to jump in and get started tailoring your LinkedIn profile to command attention to everyone lucky enough to search for you. They've made what could be a very dry subject a fun and easy, quick moving project that will quite literally change the success of your notary business.

Ignore this book and its wisdom at your own risk!

Robbie Samuels, author of *Croissants vs. Bagels: Strategic, Effective, and Inclusive Networking at Conferences* and Virtual Event Design Consultant

While this book is written specifically for mobile notary and loan signing agents, it is really for anyone who needs to think like a business owner.

LinkedIn has evolved rapidly over the last five years so it's quite likely that the profile you wrote when you first signed up is way out of date and you are not taking advantage of the power of this networking tool. This book is a great resource if you find it too overwhelming to even think about a LinkedIn strategy. Using their own business success as examples, the authors detail the steps it takes to improve your profile. Follow their advice, and your profile will turn connections into leads. You'll create a great first impression with a strong headline and back that up with a descriptive About section, recommendations, and endorsements. But that's just the start—they then show how to create strategic content leveraging the ability to now post videos, polls, and stories.

It's not just about collecting connections; it's about building a strong network. Once you've updated your profile and started posting content, you'll learn best practices for networking in this medium. Don't miss the chapter where Bill shares the mistakes he made while growing his business presence on LinkedIn. Speaking of which, one of the most under-utilized features (in my opinion) is LinkedIn Groups. I was pleased they dived into this topic so you can consider how to incorporate Groups into your networking strategy.

I have been highly recommending Sandra Long's *LinkedIn for Personal Branding: The Ultimate Guide* book for a couple of years. Bill Soroka has extensive experience in the world of mobile notaries and loan signing agents so it's perfect that they teamed up to create a book that speaks directly to their needs. Don't just read this book. Take action along the way! You'll be glad you did.

Dustin Hogan, Coach & Founder of The Rockstar Academy

This book is the perfect roadmap for leveraging the incredible power of LinkedIn to grow a successful and sustainable mobile notary and loan signing business!

The book is easy to digest and beautifully lays out the exact steps you need to take to create a LinkedIn profile that looks great AND generates business! Ultimately, growing a successful business is about building relationships that turn into clients, and this book shows you exactly how to do that using LinkedIn.

The step-by-step instructions are detailed and include real-world examples of how Bill and Sandra have used the power of LinkedIn to create incredibly successful businesses. They are candid in sharing what has worked and hasn't worked for them in the past. You will know where to focus your efforts and what pitfalls to avoid.

They left no stone unturned and finished the book with Bill's "Daily Do's." This list of daily activities will supercharge your business building efforts and make the path to success so incredibly straightforward. You'll never be wondering what to do next, and simply following these daily actions will be a gamechanger for you and your business!

Daniel C. Lewis, Executive Director/Managing Partner of Lewis Notary/Training Services Inc.

Bill Soroka has done it again. Producing another Amazon #1 Best Selling Book with LinkedIn Expert Sandra Long, this book is loaded with valuable resources and content every entrepreneur can use. This book should be considered a must read for all serious entrepreneurs that want to go to the next level.

Elizabeth C (Liz) Head – Arlington, TX, Owner of EC Head Consulting, LLC and Owner and Lead Trainer of EC Head Notary Training Workshops.

This book, *Supercharge Your Notary Business With LinkedIn*, takes us beyond the how-tos of the notary and signing agent world.

I met Bill Soroka (by phone) in November 2019. I was given *Sign & Thrive: How to Make Six Figures as a Mobile Notary and Loan Signing Agent* book at a conference. I put it in my bag! Because I was at the airport with time to kill, I picked up Bill's book instead of playing a game on my phone!!

WOW! I never picked up that phone during the wait time. As I began reading, I stopped and looked at the cover to see if I had written the book (LOL). I absolutely love connecting with like-minded people.

I found *Sign and Thrive* to be an excellent guide for notaries and have been providing it to notaries of EC Head Notary Training workshops ever since as a must read.

Now—although I read that he can be stubborn, Bill Soroka, has demonstrated that he is willing to adjust his thinking in order to add value to the notary community. This has been evidenced by his partnering with Sandra Long of *Supercharge Your Notary Business With LinkedIn.*

This book, *Supercharge Your Notary Business With LinkedIn*, has been an eye opener for me. Yes, I have been on LinkedIn for years. I have sorta-kinda used LinkedIn to say "Congratulations" when someone's anniversary or a new position is posted. I kinda-sorta kept my profile updated and did not give it much thought.

Because I have read this book, I am re-evaluating my entire LinkedIn profile and how I can use it to promote my branding for my EC Head Notary Training Workshops.

Thank you, Bill Soroka, for once again working to help all notaries be better while elevating the notary business to another level. We are not just essential during a pandemic, but every single day!

Katherine McGraw Patterson (KP), Business Strategy, Speaker, Author, Founder of WEBO Network

Bill Soroka's and Sandra Long's *Supercharge Your Notary Business With LinkedIn* is a great resource for mobile notaries (and any professional) for leveraging the leading business-to-business social media platform to attract clients. As someone who lives and breathes branding, I was impressed by the focus on building a cohesive, consistent, and intentional personal brand. In an industry that is frequently seen as a commodity, mobile notaries that take the time to set themselves apart as a business will see a resulting growth in their networks and subsequently their revenue. I will definitely be referring to Soroka and Long's advice as I work to upgrade my own LinkedIn presence.

Matt Miller, President & Founder
The California League of Independent Notaries

Supercharge Your Notary Business With LinkedIn is the very tool that Notaries need to build, optimize, and reap the rewards of a robust online social presence.

LinkedIn is the number-one personal branding tool, and this powerful guide shows you how to harness it to build connections and relationships—and stand out in your community. *Supercharge Your Notary Business With*

LinkedIn shows you step by step how to create an all-star profile and demonstrates how to successfully expand your reach by connecting with colleagues, prospects, and like-minded individuals in your area. Also, you'll learn how to become a thought leader by publishing your original content on LinkedIn's publishing network and interacting with your connections through updates and mentions.

Social Proof has never been more vital to a successful career, and this powerful new tool will make sure you don't miss out on your next big opportunity! From making connections and requesting recommendations to finding jobs and cultivating leads, this book is the guide Notaries need to take your career from good to great—all with just a few clicks.

This book will show you how to:

- Create a LinkedIn profile that showcases your skills and attracts more customers

- Find and connect with clients, colleagues, and industry leaders

- Understand LinkedIn etiquette and best practices

- Use LinkedIn to find jobs, develop connections, and market your services

Stay competitive and relevant—read this book to learn how to benefit from the Internet's authority in professional networking.

DEDICATION

To you, who believes in this work you do as a mobile notary and loan signing agent enough to pick up a book like this, read it, and apply it. This work really does matter. And if we want to elevate the field, we have to elevate the game.

HOW TO USE THIS BOOK

The book you hold in your hands is a blueprint to optimizing your LinkedIn profile, creating the valuable content your audience is craving, and getting in the "arena" and connecting with the exact people you have identified as your ideal customer.

It's more than that too. When you're proud of your LinkedIn profile, your confidence is boosted. You might even have a little 'swagger' in your step just knowing that when someone searches for you on LinkedIn or the internet at large, they're going to find information that you curated to be sure your best self is face forward.

Every strategy and tip we offer in this book can be implemented with the *free* version of LinkedIn. This does not *require* an upgrade to LinkedIn Premium.

There's a lot at stake here, so we encourage you to take this book seriously. Use it as the tool it was designed for.

- Read it.

- Implement as you go. Don't trust yourself to read through it first and then come back later and do the work. Let's do this together and right this minute!

- If you have the print edition, the greatest gift you could give yourself is to bend the pages, highlight, underline, and make notes in the margins. That's what textbooks are for—learning!

If you want to keep a separate, "pretty" copy, we have options on the Reader's Resource Website. In fact, you'll find lots of free resources on that resource website, including:

- Over 52 Notary-specific topics to create content around

- The Morning Mastery Mini-course from Bill

- Links to incredible organizations, groups, and associations that will support you along your journey

- A Canva course to help you create free and easy social media graphics

- And so much more!

- You can access all of that at www.NotaryCoach.com/linkedin

- Enjoy the read and be sure to connect with us on LinkedIn

BEFORE YOU BEGIN...

Let's take a results inventory of where you're at with LinkedIn right now. It's important to know your starting point so you can track your progress, adjust your strategy, and celebrate your wins.

If you're reading the e-book version of this book, write these numbers in a journal, a calendar, or even just a sticky-note.

It's difficult to track the full impact of your LinkedIn presence and the relationships it will cultivate, but the numbers below will give you a tangible baseline and measurable results from your efforts directly from this book.

These numbers can be found throughout your LinkedIn account, including the Profile section and your Dashboard.

	Now	After Implemen- tation	1 Year later
# of Connections			
# of Profile Views			
# of Monthly Posts			
# of Recommendations Given			
# of Recommendations Received			
# of Search Appearances			
# of Followers			

DISCLAIMER

We wrote this book to help you establish brand reputation, deliver valuable content to your audience, and connect with your ideal customers. As much as we believe in each and every one of you, we can't guarantee results. We make no promises about income, connections, or any other results.

And, of course, the standard: We are not attorneys; therefore, we cannot and are not providing legal advice, nor are we permitted to collect fees for any legal advice.

INTRODUCTION FROM BILL

Did you roll your eyes a little bit when you saw the title of this book, *Supercharge Your Notary Business With LinkedIn?* I can totally relate if you did, because I was a resistor too. If you didn't roll your eyes, maybe you immediately see the incredible value of LinkedIn for your mobile notary and loan signing business, which makes you WAY smarter than I am.

As seems to be the trend in my life, I can be a bit stubborn, and I tend to resist those things I need the most, and LinkedIn is one of those things my business and I needed the most.

I am delighted to be able to share my experience with LinkedIn with you for just that reason. Its power for today's mobile notary and loan signing agent is obvious to some, and yet to others is oblivious (that was me!).

My wakeup call(s) came from a few different directions. Even the most direct of which, "your LinkedIn profile sucked," didn't prompt a change in my LinkedIn behavior. I'll share that story later in this book.

The inspiration to finally take my LinkedIn profile and strategy more seriously came from a referral in another book. You see, that's what I do when I need to figure something out—I read a book about it. And I don't even remember which book it was that referred me to Sandra Long's book, *LinkedIn For Personal Branding: The Ultimate Guide.* I am just glad it did!

Following the steps of Sandra's book changed the face of my company and my branding forever. Now, instead of LinkedIn being some random and dated resume, it became my calling card. I've had three direct clients tell me that they hired me *because* of my LinkedIn presence. Regardless of my marketing skills or signing presence, they researched me likely on Google, which inevitably displayed my LinkedIn profile.

Thanks to what I learned from Sandra Long, that profile represented my best self and landed me those clients. And over time, those three clients' revenue have totaled hundreds of thousands of dollars in signing revenue.

As you read this book, my wish is that you will implement as you go. LinkedIn is not some magic pill that will instantly turn your business around or suddenly provide you with the multiple six-figure income you daydream about. But over time, or maybe faster than you expect, you will meet the very person or persons who will help make all your dreams come true. How does it happen? It's a combination of things, of course. Many of which Sandra and I will lay out for you here in this book.

Still, the biggest component of your success in business and with LinkedIn comes from one essential philosophy from the late and great Zig Ziglar: "If you help enough people get what they want, you will get what you want."

Come from a genuine place of service and authenticity, and you can't ever go wrong.

Everything you're building on LinkedIn is bigger than your current circumstances. Yes, it will help you grow your mobile notary and loan signing business of course (that's why we're all here, right?). But there's something bigger at work here too. We're always "becoming" something as we grow and evolve.

You may absolutely *love* your notary business, so it may very well be your *last* business. Congrats to you if that's the case! And you may also outgrow your notary business, or add more services to it, or just plain move on.

The results you get from all this effort you put in on LinkedIn right now goes with you—it serves you now and in the future—no matter what you may do down the road. This is *your* audience. If they trust you now in this business, they'll trust you again in the next.

Always keep your mind on the big picture and plan for long-term relationships that last no matter what business you are in.

INTRODUCTION FROM SANDRA

I am not a notary myself, but now I know dozens of them around the USA thanks to Bill Soroka. A few years ago, I got a LinkedIn message from Bill. He was reading my book *LinkedIn for Personal Branding: The Ultimate Guide* and wanted to connect. He told me that he felt LinkedIn was crucial for the notaries he was coaching, and he loved my book. Who doesn't love flattery? Who doesn't love Bill Soroka?

We started talking. One thing led to another. We did some webinars for his notary community and introduced them to my *LinkedIn Club*. We recently decided to co-author this book. We are both passionate about helping notaries succeed. He knows all about how to build a successful, thriving notary business, and I know all about LinkedIn.

I have learned so much from Bill. He explained that many notaries are entering the business because self-employment is so attractive now. Many notaries seem to have multiple gigs or be in the process of transforming their lives. Bill's biggest thrill is helping a notary skyrocket their income & lifestyle, creating a legacy they can be proud of. I am excited to be a part of his vision when it comes to *Supercharge Your Notary Business With LinkedIn*. I want LinkedIn to be a fabulous tool in the notary toolbelt.

To every notary public starting this book, I say WELCOME! We are so glad you are here to learn how LinkedIn can help you build your brand, grow your network, and increase your business opportunities!

CHAPTER 1

WHY LINKEDIN FOR NOTARIES

Much of this book was written to help you put your best face forward to your potential clients and to the public in general.

Why did we set it up that way?

Besides the obvious importance of personal branding and marketing, it comes down to self-confidence. Your stellar, or as Sandra so aptly calls it, "Sizzlin" profile on LinkedIn WILL open doors of communication and relationships you may not have even thought about yet.

Having an optimized LinkedIn profile absolutely WILL help you get found online by the very people that need and appreciate your services.

All of this is true.

And we're going to suggest that having a LinkedIn profile that is a real, authentic representation of you, the value you bring to the marketplace, the impact you want to have on the community you serve, and the legacy you want to leave behind when you're gone, is more important than all of that other stuff.

When you have a LinkedIn profile that you are proud of, it changes how you show up in the world. It changes how you have conversations with people. It changes what you post online. It helps you be who you want to be in this world. It emboldens you to take steps you may not have otherwise taken because you know exactly what people will find when they research you. You've controlled the narrative!

LinkedIn isn't just another social media platform. It is your business card, your resume, your website, blog and vlog, and your call to action all rolled into one.

LinkedIn matters. And to the extent that you optimize it and utilize it in and for your day to day business, it will enhance your business, relationships, and revenue to levels you're only dreaming about right now.

Imagine if there was just one place where everyone you might consider your ideal or perfect client hung out every week and shared the stuff that is important to them.

That place is LinkedIn.

Who, then, is *your* ideal client?

Who is Your Ideal Customer?

Throughout this book, we will be using the words "customer," "prospect," "client," and "audience" synonymously. We are doing that because, depending on your business model, you might call them by different names. Don't let that hang you up. Choose the noun that works for you and apply this knowledge to your business.

Having a clear understanding of who your ideal customer is will help you tailor your content and messaging as you implement the strategies in this book. This is extremely important, and I urge you not to skip this step of identifying your ideal customer.

Many notaries who do not get this clarity on who their audience is slip into what is easy for them, like talking to other notaries with their social media and LinkedIn content. They share their training wins, frustrations with customers or the Secretary of State, or even their income milestones. If you are intending to be a notary influencer or trainer, that would make total sense. But the ideal customer for most notaries is *not* other notaries. It's actually customers and clients that may pay for their services.

So, let's get clear on that first. For *your* business as a mobile notary and loan signing agent, who are likely candidates for your ideal customers? Your particular business model, like whether you are pursuing general notary work (Specialty Notary Work) and/or loan signings, will make a difference in this, but here are a few ideas to get you started:

- Signing companies
- Escrow officers
- Escrow branch managers
- Escrow business development managers
- Real estate attorneys
- Closing agents
- Mortgage loan officers
- Estate planning attorneys
- Real estate agents
- Skilled nursing facility managers
- Senior living community managers
- Tow yard managers

One of the beautiful things about this business is the additional streams of service and revenue you can add on, often referred to as side hustles. Let's look at a couple of the common ones we see for notaries and describe some of their ideal customers too.

For wedding officiants, some of your ideal customers might be:

- Recently engaged individuals or couples
- Wedding planners
- Event venue managers
- Wedding resource guide managers or publishers

- Other wedding officiants

For fingerprinting technicians, some of your ideal customers might be:

- The local Bar Association

- School administrators

- Hospital administrators

- Local law enforcement agencies

It comes down to this—who do you want to attract and/or engage with? That's the question you want to answer and have on the forefront of your mind as you proceed with the rest of this book.

Once you've dialed in your audience, you'll know exactly what to say and how to present yourself.

DID YOU ACCESS THE
RESOURCES WEBSITE YET?

GET FREE ACCESS AT
www.NotaryCoach.com/linkedin

CHAPTER 2

PERSONAL BRANDING FOR NOTARIES

Being known as an excellent, reliable notary will prompt people to seek you out. Today's consumers are asking their peers for notary recommendations. According to Sandra, "Personal branding drives an increase in referrals and specifically attracts people to you."

SUPERCHARGER TIP

As soon as your name is mentioned or referred, expect people to view your LinkedIn profile for further validation.

Personal branding is the act of strategically managing your image and defining your unique value. In many circles, especially within the Search Engine Optimization (SEO) communities, this is known as *Brand Rep* or *Brand Reputation*. It impacts your prospect's and client's impressions of you and your

21

business. If you don't work on this proactively, expect that there can be a wrong turn as people might not appreciate your full value.

Wrong Turn Example: Your client is at a Chamber of Commerce event where he is asked about good local notaries. He provides your name along with one other. The prospect looks for you on LinkedIn and can't find you. He finds the other notary and contacts her. Ouch!

You don't create your personal brand. It's more about knowing yourself and demonstrating your best genuine self rather than creating anything new. You don't want to be fabricating a false impression or presence. This is all about authenticity. In addition to experience and skills, personal branding may incorporate *your personality, passion, drives, values, and vision.* Brands vary widely as we are not all carbon copies of each other. In the notary world, your individual personality is one of your key differentiators. We tend to emphasize or be known for certain things over others.

Your brand may include many of the more "intangible" aspects in addition to your experience and skills. Think about yourself: What are the unique qualities or values that apply to you? People hire notaries for more than their licenses, education, or experiences. This is true for all business today.

Think about the last time you hired an attorney, realtor, or other professional. Did you pick him or her because of her company or college OR did you look for specific personal attributes such as detail-oriented, trust-worthy, or discreet?

Trust and Integrity

The role of the notary is one that requires impeccable trust and integrity at all times. *Wikipedia* describes the value as the following: "Documents are notarized to deter fraud and to ensure they are properly executed." In short, *this work matters*! Major transactions and life decisions are hinging on this trust. Fortunes are transferred, rights are granted and revoked, responsibilities are bestowed and taken away—all with the swipe of your pen and an impression of your notary seal.

The funny thing is, people judge your trustworthiness based on your reputation and their first impressions of you both online AND offline. Your potential customers will work with who they know, like, and trust. Fortunately, LinkedIn is a valuable digital space where you can solidify an impression and build that trust.

Brand Impressions: The Evidence

Your brand is demonstrated in many ways and places. Think about all the factors that impact other people's impressions of you as a professional. Your brand attributes are evident online in areas such as:

- Website

- Google search

- Zoom meetings

- Reviews

- Blog posts

- Social media

- Email content

- Podcasts

- Radio

- YouTube Videos

Your brand is also evident in your business cards, brochures, proposals, letters, articles, and presentations if you have a physical location that is also representative of your brand.

Your *personal live activity* makes an impact on your brand. You are making a brand impression while you are at:

- Networking events

- Signings and other notary appointments

- Community events

- Volunteering

- Toastmasters or other organizations

- Notary meetups

This book focuses on using LinkedIn to establish and enhance your brand image, thought leadership, and credibility as a notary. We will also show you ways to connect with your ideal customers. It's a good idea to consider all of the other ways to display the key elements of your brand and have those be consistent with your LinkedIn profile.

In fact, if you use your LinkedIn profile as your main "base-profile," all of your other online profiles can be derived from it. Think how easy it will be to pull out relevant and stellar content from LinkedIn to populate your notary directory profiles!

SUPERCHARGER TIP

Your brand attributes include your expertise, attitude, values, approaches, interests, and likeability. Your brand evidence is online and offline!

Your Notary Brand

Be an extraordinary notary, and your brand will shine. Take your business seriously enough to get trained. No more "winging it." Learn all you can about your functions as a Notary Public, the customers you serve, and how YOU show up to each transaction and to life in general. That gives you *plenty* to learn—always. Forever be the student. Know your strengths. Know your weaknesses. Prioritize your learning and skill building. And above all else, remember your two main responsibilities:

- Expertly perform the duties you have been hired to perform and in integrity with all laws and guidelines for your state.

- And lay the foundation for a relationship that will last beyond this one single transaction.

That's how you grow a relationship-based business. We absolutely MUST grow through the "transaction" mindset and into the "relationship" mindset. Remembering these two main responsibilities will help you create a business that will thrive in *any* economy.

Being successful on LinkedIn is not just about being successful online. Your online presence needs to complement everything you are doing in the real world as a notary. So, as you progress in your notary business, make sure you are sharing it, writing about it, speaking about it, or helping others. Share your journey!

Much of the work that you do is a great demonstration and validation of your strengths. It is up to you to be an amazing notary, to differentiate yourself, and to become memorable. It is up to you to display this as your brand.

Your customers may not know it at first (because most of the general public doesn't fully understand the function of a Notary Public), but they are *craving* an expert who knows exactly how to help them. Become that expert. Know your state laws. Get ongoing training and support that keeps you dialed in to the industry and ever-changing notary landscape. Know the resources you can lean on when you don't know the answer. Being resourceful and knowing where to find the answers also makes you the expert.

Experts are Continuous Learners

Being a top-notch notary will also mean you are a continuous learner. Bill subscribes to the Japanese philosophy of Kaizen, which is constant, continuous improvement, as he discusses in his book *Sign and Thrive: How to Make Six Figures as a Mobile Notary and Loan Signing Agent.*

Part of your learning is merely staying up to date on the most current trends, laws, and news. Set up a Google Alert on the most relevant notary specific topics so you are reading the latest news every day. Be an active participant and perhaps even a member with the *National Notary Association.* Join online communities such as those offered by *Notary Coach, Notary2Pro, Safe Haven for New Notaries, the Tuesday Notary Titans Call,* and more to keep and stay up to date in the notary industry. As with any business, there are many skills necessary to succeed. It's not all about the laws and notarial duties. Running a notary business requires skills in marketing, bookkeeping, advertising, relationships, social media, and more. Consider other online learning communities too, such as the *LinkedIn Personal Best Club*, to stay current with LinkedIn. The best experts are continuous learners. Learn how to master your craft and grow your business as a continual process.

Check out our resource website for a list of additional resources you can tap into.

It's About You as a Person

Your brand is more than just your certifications and years of experience. It's an intangible asset and your strategic advantage. Your personal brand is a combination of many of your personal attributes, skills, and qualities. It's the invisible elements of your presence that make you unique. Your brand also incorporates your personality, values, vision, passions, goals, and strategic focus.

Not all notaries are equal. This is true regarding your expertise as well as the most intangible aspects of your brand. Figure out how you can differentiate yourself from everyone else. It might be what you know or how you approach a problem. It might be your unique personal qualities that make a difference. The important thing to remember is that as a solo-preneur, there is no separation between you and your business. *Everything* you post online, along with every interaction you have with a human being, both while on assignment or off, is a reflection of your brand. Use this insight to help you grow and become the best version of yourself for that.

The Four Pillars of Your Relationship-Based Business

As you build your brand and establish your reputation both online and through your business practices, there are four components—or pillars—to which everything else you do will be reliant.

First, let's talk about competence. Competence is your ability to perform your duties knowledgeably. This is where having training makes all the difference, especially when you aim to go above and beyond in your duties presenting documents, as in loan signing and living trust appointments. This is also where skills on printing and other equipment, invoicing, reliable vehicles, and knowing who to call and when with questions, resides.

The second pillar is your confidence factor. This is essentially how you demonstrate your abilities. Confidence often shines through the words you choose to use, the way you take what Carol Ray of Notary2Pro calls "gentle control" of your appointments, whether or not you look your clients in the eye when speaking, and a whole host of other attributes.

Integrity is our third pillar. Integrity can be defined in many ways, but in the world of the notary, here's a short and sweet definition: do what you said you would do. Sounds simple enough, but let's really dig into this for a minute.

When you think about all the agreements you make as a mobile notary and loan signing agent, it might not be as simple of a definition. Think about these:

- In order to have become a Notary Public in your state, you have agreed to abide by the rules, laws, and guidelines of that state.

- If you have opted to become a National Notary Association Certified Loan Signing Agent, then you have agreed to abide by the accepted Code of Conduct.

- If you tell someone you will be somewhere at 9:00am, be there and ready to perform at 9:00am. It's not just courtesy; it is integrity.

And finally, our fourth pillar is likeability.

Just like Bill says in *Sign & Thrive: How to Make Six Figures as a Mobile Notary and Loan Signing Agent,* "People work with people who they like, know, and trust. Whether we agree with it or not, likeability is probably the biggest factor here. You could be strong in all three of the other pillars. Maybe you're great at what you do and how you do it. Perhaps you may be confident in those abilities and know how to take gentle control of signing. And maybe you have impeccable integrity too. But if you are a real jerk to work with, you'll be out of business in no time."

Do You Specialize? Or Do Multiple Jobs?

It's much harder to be considered an expert of twenty things. Be selective and focus intensely on a couple of things. Yes, you may have multiple gigs as a notary, and we discuss this in-depth in later chapters; however, if you are doing numerous things, it is all the more reason to be CLEAR. Your clarity will attract people once they understand your role or roles. Now take your brand a step further with your personal qualities. Here are some examples of how we might be described by others:

- A mobile notary who cares about the needs of seniors as they plan their estates and take care of their families.

- A loan signing agent that truly cares about the success of their clients and consistently hosts or promotes networking events to help them get more referrals.

- A virtual assistant who is certified in Remote Online Notarization so they are truly full-service.

- A jubilant notary that makes every appointment enjoyable and professional and is also a dynamic wedding officiant.

- A mobile notary and loan signing agent that shares their journey and mentors new notaries on their business growth

How will people describe YOU? What do you want them to say about you?

Be Yourself and Build Professional Friendships

Advice from Sandra Long in *LinkedIn for Personal Branding: The Ultimate Guide*: "Be your best professional self, and clients and employers are bound to be attracted to you. Your unique perspectives and viewpoints will serve as a magnet. People online want to know people *like you* with thoughtful opinions and helpful content. When you are authentic and true to yourself, your values shine through. Yes, you will attract your ideal prospects and repel people who are not suited to be part of your community. And this is OK!"

Demonstrate Rather Than Boast

Rather than using LinkedIn to boast about your accomplishments, focus on demonstrating your expertise. So instead of SAYING you are a notary expert, show it! You can do this by displaying your certifications, organizational affiliations, work experience, and content. Your prospective clients will want to work with you if you are focused on their success. Be the helpful notary expert, and paths will lead to you. In sharing your passionate journey, bring the value!

Be Proactive

Decide exactly who you are, what you wish to emphasize, and then make it happen on LinkedIn and elsewhere! Don't leave it to chance to think that you are *known* already. You are in control of a large portion of the perspective that people have of you. You control your personal brand by the combination of your live actions and corresponding online profile. Yes, spend time crafting a wonderful LinkedIn profile and then keeping it up to date always.

This takes commitment. One post every now and again does NOT do the trick. You have to stay consistent. Remember, your ideal customers—your audience—are busy. They are not sitting in front of their computer, eagerly anticipating your next kernel of information or wisdom to be dropped on LinkedIn. As a business owner on a mission, it is your responsibility to keep yourself top of mind with your potential clients. In the following chapters, we're going to show you how to do just that.

Are You Ready for Your LinkedIn Profile?

Think first about your best authentic self as you prepare to write your entire LinkedIn profile. This evolving self-perception of your brand should guide you as you go through the profile writing process.

Quick Exercise: Jot down all the words that describe your personal values. As you are working on your profile, consider how your values might shine through and attract your prospects.

Let's now move to the next chapter, where we will learn how to get started on your LinkedIn profile.

CHAPTER 3

LINKEDIN PROFILE START-UP!

You are on LinkedIn to develop opportunities and relationships. This starts with being found easily. We want clients, prospects, industry connections, and friends to find us online.

Make sure your profile leaves someone thinking, "I am impressed" or "I have to meet this person as soon as possible!" or "We need a notary like this!"

Use Language to Your Advantage

Language helps you to be found and creates impressions, so select your words carefully and for the most significant impact. These language suggestions impact your brand too. Our recommended language can be used throughout your LinkedIn profile.

Language Tip 1: First Person

Write your LinkedIn profile using the first person tense. This means using the words *I* and *My* instead of *Sandra* and *Bill.* This is considered friendlier and more approachable. It also allows you to tell a story. You can write with the first person without boasting, especially if you focus on how you help your clients and why you love what you do.

Language Tip 2: Keywords

Keywords are what your potential clients and customers are using to search for you and your services. These keywords are usually affiliated with search engines like Google and Bing and are a critical element to Search Engine Optimization (SEO). But SEO and keywords work far broader than just traditional websites and search engines. You can use keywords on ALL of your online profiles and content to help your potential clients find you. People may find you on LinkedIn based on the words you select for your profile. Keywords should be an accurate reflection of you, your experience, and your brand. Consider what you want to be found for and what you want to be hired for. Here are some example keywords for notaries:

- Notary

- Notary Public

- Mobile Notary

- Notary Signing Agent

- Remote Online Notary

- Online Notary

- Traveling Notary

- Loan Signing Agent

- Mortgage

- Reverse Mortgage

Consider using your keywords throughout your LinkedIn profile, but make sure the wording sounds natural and is an accurate portrayal of your capabilities. The keywords are incredibly powerful when located in your headline and job titles. Other useful sections in which to use keywords are the About essay, Skills, Experience, Volunteering, and the Credibility sections.

Language Tip 3: Action Verbs

Use strong action verbs to describe your accomplishments. For your current role, use present tense. For your past positions, use the past tense. Here are some examples of action verbs (in the past tense) for notaries:

- Completed
- Created
- Developed
- Officiated
- Notarized
- Signed
- Finalized
- Transacted
- Closed
- Wrote
- Initiated
- Spoke
- Taught

The Power of Search: Google and LinkedIn

The Google search algorithm ranks the LinkedIn website very highly, so not having a profile is a massive disadvantage for today's professional notary. Some notaries and other business owners now open their practice with a LinkedIn profile before building a company website. Your LinkedIn profile can be found directly from Google if you have optimized it with keywords and relevant content.

SUPERCHARGER TIP
The Google search algorithm ranks the LinkedIn website very highly, so an optimized profile will likely appear in top search results.

Let's be clear—optimizing all of your online content, including your LinkedIn profile, for search engines is absolutely critical to grow a sustainable business. Your potential clients *must* be able to find you. Because search engines like Google & Bing consider LinkedIn an "authority" site, refining and optimizing your profile and adding fresh content will certainly help more and more people find you through searches on those platforms.

You can also be found through the LinkedIn search by name, company, geography, or even keywords related to your specialties. So it makes sense to use the words that are most appropriate for your business, practice, or career. Being specific is optimal. For a notary, keywords such as "notary," "loan," "mortgage," "documents," or "loan signing agent" are good options.

Using the right keywords is not only a search strategy. You want to choose words that resonate with your potential clients. Speaking the right "industry language" can make a difference in how comfortable your client is with you once you have been found. So we believe that the words you choose can be compelling for both reasons. Previously, we gave you some examples of common keywords you may want to incorporate into your profile and content. Additionally, you may consider using other words and phrases that the general public may use. These can vary a bit because the majority of people don't know exactly what a notary does or why they exist. They don't always know exactly what they need. That means their search terms could be far different than what you might expect as an industry practitioner.

Think about this search power. LinkedIn has very high Search Engine Optimization (SEO) ranking authority with Google. Once your profile is optimized, you can expect your LinkedIn profile to rank higher than most of the other content displayed on Google. You want your LinkedIn profile to become the main focal point for any online search. That's why it is so important to get your profile to a place where you are absolutely proud of it, and it is representative of your best self.

Now, let's talk a little bit about another facet of "brand rep." Sometimes, people say things about us online that are not very nice, whether true or not. Protecting your brand's reputation helps make sure your business survives, even if a few negative situations or comments spring up. In the unlikely event that your name is ever associated with malicious online articles, comments, or reviews, those posts usually appear lower on a Google search page once your profile is complete and optimized.

SUPERCHARGER TIP

In the unlikely event that your name is ever associated with malicious online articles, comments, or reviews, those posts usually appear lower on Google search page results once your LinkedIn profile is complete and optimized.

There are still some things you can do now to help minimize the risk of negative content coming up during a search of your name or business. Take the time now also to clean up any harmful Facebook, Twitter, Instagram, or YouTube activity. Remove posts that will embarrass you later. Fortunately, you can count on your LinkedIn profile to rise high in Google ranking and represent your best professional self. Having a *complete* profile is the primary starting point to accomplish *being found* online.

Google and other search engines "like" LinkedIn, so your properly optimized and relevant LinkedIn profile will likely appear higher in search results than most other online content.

Bill's LinkedIn profile appears just below his website and course, but above his book, YouTube, Instagram, and other online links are visible. LinkedIn is clearly near the top of Bill's digital presence.

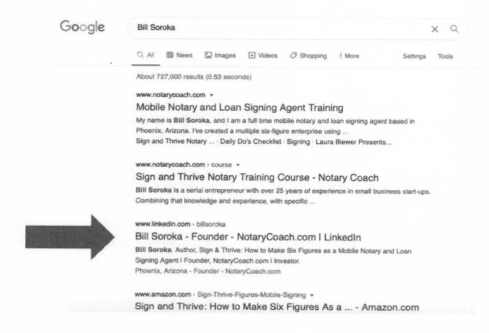

SUPERCHARGER TIP

Make sure your profile is fully visible on Google by making it "Public." Find this in the Public Profile visibility setting under Privacy.

Be an All-Star Notary on LinkedIn ☆

LinkedIn has a measurement for profile completeness. Aim for an All-Star status, which is their top designation. LinkedIn will prompt you to the next step if you aren't an All-Star now. Keep in mind, however, that this meter doesn't address the **quality** of content on your profile. So become an All-Star, but don't stop there! Be sure to follow the recommendations in this book to be an All-Star Notary on LinkedIn. The minimum requirements include the following:

- your industry and location

- an up-to-date current position (with a description)

- two past positions

- your education

- your skills (minimum of three)

- a profile photo

- at least fifty connections

Broadcast Your New Notary Position?

LinkedIn allows you to push out a notification to your network if you have updated sections of your profile. Sandra calls this *broadcasting*. If you have a new notary position, this is an excellent way to get the word out to your network. However, if you are just cleaning things up and adding in older or previous positions, you may decide not to make a public announcement. If you wish to temporarily shut off or turn on this notification, first go to Privacy and Settings, which you will find under the ME tab. Under the Privacy tab, select *Sharing job changes, education changes, and work anniversaries from your profile*, and then select your desired setting.

Your Name

People will search for you by name on both LinkedIn and Google. Most Google searches for names lead to a LinkedIn profile. If your name is common, the search result will show all the people with your exact name, so it's best if your profile is complete because it's more likely to rise to the top. Being connected will also help your name rise to the top of a name search.

SUPERCHARGER TIP
Most Google searches for an individual name
will lead to a LinkedIn profile.

Be aware that LinkedIn is very strict about the name field. **Do not add keywords, phone numbers, or a URL in the name field**. It also looks incorrect and makes it harder for the name search.

Display only your real name that you use in your notary business on your LinkedIn profile. Don't use the LinkedIn personal profile for a company, organization, or group. The personal profile page is designed for a real person only.

SUPERCHARGER TIP
Display ONLY Your Real Name in the "name" field. Do NOT use a
business name for a personal profile.

Make sure your full name is spelled correctly and consistently across your other social media, résumé, bios, and websites. The first letter of your first and last name should be capitalized. All other letters should be lower case. Don't use all upper or lower case. Using all uppercase letters online is synonymous with shouting.

You may wish to show a maiden or former name in the name field. If LinkedIn users may be looking for you using your previous name, then by all means, show it. Edit the name field and add the former name under the *Former Name* section. This is an example of the LinkedIn display:

Jessica (Miller) Smith

You are currently permitted to add your certifications or suffixes in the name field after your last name. Use this if you believe your credentials are specifically being used in a search. Simply add the accreditation after the last name field.

Example:

John Smith MSW

Also, make sure you add the details of your special designations in the Licenses and Certifications section as described in Chapter 7.

Industry and Location

At the top of your profile, you have an opportunity to declare your location and industry. Take the time to make the right choices. For the industry designation, you will need to select from the options provided from the drop-down menu that LinkedIn offers. Most notaries will select *legal services* for the industry.

For the location, there are two options based on your unique local postal code. Typically, by entering your postal or city code, most of us choose either the local town or the greater metropolitan area. We recommend selecting the major metropolitan area near you unless you are laser-focused on ONE specific village or community.

Here's how we did it:

Name	Local Postal Code	Choice A	Choice B	Displays
Sandra	06880	Westport CT	New York City Metropolitan Area	New York City Metropolitan Area
Bill	85013	Phoenix AZ	Greater Phoenix Area	Greater Phoenix Area

If you are a notary covering the state, county, or region, select the larger city. Many of us will choose the large metropolitan area if we are looking for clients in the broader geography.

Customize Your URL

LinkedIn gives users an opportunity for a customized URL corresponding to your individual profile. We recommend choosing a URL that is as close to your name as possible. You will have your own URL for the profile page, which is more attractive if you customize it.

Example of a URL likely to be assigned by LinkedIn:

www.linkedin.com/in/bill-soroka-c765aa2

Example of a customized URL:

www.linkedin.com/in/billsoroka

Why customize this? Because it gives you the opportunity to:

- have a more attractive professional link

- use it on your email signature, website, and business cards

- improve search hits

- remember easily and share with others

What's the best URL? We recommend you try to get your exact first and last name just like Bill Soroka did. Keep in mind there are no spaces or capital letters. Don't select a company name for your URL.

If your name is more common like Sandra Long, it's very possible that your first choice for the vanity URL will not be available. Consider adding a middle initial or listing your last name followed by first name. Also, LinkedIn will recommend alternative versions for you to consider. For many of us with common names, you will have to choose the best alternative. Whatever you choose is likely to be far better than the URL assigned automatically by LinkedIn.

Contact Information

Fill out the Contact Info section entirely because some people will go there to get your pertinent details to reach you. In the Contact Info section, add your personal or company websites, phone number, and work address if you have one. Go to settings to enter your email and Twitter handle, and then they will automatically display under the Contact Info section.

Your prospects may want to call or email you directly after viewing your profile, so make it easy for them to find this information. We also suggest adding your contact information at the bottom of your About essay too, and letting people know how to contact or follow you is a top priority for most of us. This last piece is also known as a "Call to Action" or CTA. This is where you literally tell your readers exactly what action you want them to take. What do you want them to do? Call you? Email you? Text you? Visit your website? You name it!

Featured Section: Display Your Best Content or Work Samples

There is a new profile segment called the Featured section, where you can showcase work samples, brochures, videos, and documents in a very prominent part of your profile. You can now feature or pin posts that you've authored or re-shared, articles you've published on LinkedIn, and even external media such as images, documents, and links.

Here is some of Bill's *featured* content—he shares several of his YouTube videos.

Featured

Notary Reviews Founder Carrie Rivera is our Dyno-Mite Special Guest on TNT 1-22-19
YouTube

Tuesday Notary Titans (TNT) is like an old fashioned radio call-in show, but for notaries just like you...and with full video so we can all see each other (i...

Real Estate Agent Leverages Contacts & Experience to Grow a Mobile Notary and Loan Signing Business
YouTube

Profiles in Ink: Mr. Bill Bumphrey If you are a real estate agent, or previous real estate agent, your experience could be valuable if you look to grow an ad...

5 Phases of becoming a mobile notary and signing agent for the mortgage industry
YouTube

This section is the best profile improvement in a decade. Take advantage of the Featured section!

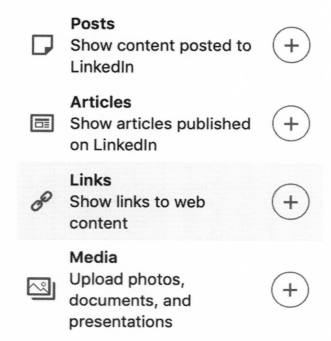

Imagine the possibilities for notaries!

- Image of you at an appointment or otherwise with a client
- Image of your commission certificate *(check your state laws)*
- Link to a YouTube video of you talking about why you are a notary
- LinkedIn post or article which highlights your values (confidentiality, efficiency, or timeliness) or your thought leadership
- Image of you volunteering in your community
- Image of you at a national or state notary conference
- Travel images or the lengths you go for your customers

LinkedIn Profile Start-Up!

The images, links, and rich media that you select for your LinkedIn Featured section should be just as strategic as the words and language. Use this section to share more about yourself and have fun!

CHAPTER 4

BEDROCK: EXPERIENCE AND EDUCATION

LinkedIn is the best place to attract and motivate prospects and clients online. Be sure to take the time to update your current experience section to become specifically relevant for clients and prospects. Perhaps your profile hasn't been updated since you became a notary. In other words, your profile is possibly *recruiter facing* or more like a *resume, as if you are job hunting,* instead of focusing on how you help notary customers! What do your prospects think when they arrive at your page and read your experience section? This requires a shift from "employee thinking" to "entrepreneur thinking."

Make sure your experience section clearly explains how you help notary clients. You may want to describe the clients or geography that you serve. Add a brief company description too.

The LinkedIn professional experience section is incredibly powerful because of these unique attributes:

- It helps you to be found. Your experience title, location, and description are all great SEO attraction spots on your profile. You can also add relevant keywords after your title or in the description.

- Work examples or *professional portfolio*. For each Experience section, you have the opportunity to upload work samples such as videos, images, or presentations.

- Nesting or Position grouping. LinkedIn now groups your experience sections under one employer for a cleaner look.

- Company logos and links. Your profile may have a company logo, and this becomes a direct link to the company's page (the page is set up separately).

- Flexible display order. Display your most relevant experience first, so it will be highlighted at the top of your profile.

- Can help you blend other gigs, services, and side hustles

Your work experience is a critical section of your LinkedIn profile because it is a tangible representation of what you do and how you help your clients. Make it compelling by writing in the first person. It is also a great place to use language and keywords that are notary specific and attractive to your prospects.

For each position that you list in the Experience section, include the title, company name, location, dates, and description. Label your work as Full-Time, Part-Time, Self-Employed, Freelance, Contract, Internship, or Apprenticeship. Most notaries are self-employed, but you may also enjoy a freelance or contract position with a larger organization.

Current and Past Experience

List multiple positions, including those that are current and past. In most cases, it is wise to list all your jobs, titles, locations, dates, and descriptions of these in your LinkedIn profile. People may decide to connect with you if they are reminded that you were once coworkers by seeing your early experiences on your profile. You never know what people will relate too! Plus, remember that all of your previous experience has brought you here today. All of that will serve you well in your role as a mobile notary and loan signing agent. LinkedIn recommends displaying your current role and the past two positions at a minimum.

SUPERCHARGER TIP

Include current and past experiences in your profile. People who you worked with at a previous job may be looking for you OR refer you now as a notary.

Display the Logo Associated with Each Experience

When you add a company name, select it from the drop-down menu if the organization has a company page on LinkedIn. If they have a page but you still don't see their logo on your profile after you select them, simply delete the name and reenter it and select the drop-down choice to secure the logo. This logo is also a link to that company's page. Always remember that if you are an employee, your personal profile is also an extension of your employer's brand.

For your current role as a mobile notary and loan signing agent, we will touch on how to build a company page for your business on LinkedIn in a later chapter.

SUPERCHARGER TIP

If you are self-employed and don't yet have a company page, select *self-employed* for the type of experience, and LinkedIn will give you a logo-type image in place of a company logo.

Always Fill Out the Description in the Experience Section

One common mistake is leaving the description blank. Don't miss this valuable opportunity.

Use the experience section to share how you help clients in your business. It should be crystal clear in this section as to the what, who, and where of your business. Also consider adding a short sentence about your company. We like to think of this as the *meat and potatoes* section.

This is also another opportunity in both your current and former experience sections to sprinkle in more keywords that will help boost your rankings in LinkedIn and on search engines.

Example:

Bill's NotaryBlu Description:

We LOVE what we do, and we do it ANYWHERE, and ANYTIME. Being a stellar Signing Agent means more than knowing what documents to sign and date. We make sure we show up on time, communicate, build rapport, have a little fun, and ensure smooth and efficient signings EVERY time. At NotaryBlu, we recognize that we are an extension of our Escrow Officer and real estate professional clients in every way—personality, standard of excellence, and work ethic. NotaryBlu—It's Smooth Signings From Here!

SUPERCHARGER TIP

A LinkedIn profile should NOT be the same as a résumé. It should be a valuable marketing page for you and your notary business!

Portfolio Career: Many Notaries Have Multiple Gigs!

More and more people are working multiple jobs while also developing a notary business. Some of today's workers are creating a patchwork of contract work and jobs. We recommend that you list all relevant experience on your profile. Your "About" essay will be the key to how you spin all of this together successfully. It's also the best place to explain your priorities. We'll dive deeper into that in Chapter 6.

We are seeing a wide variety of work experiences now. Here are some possible combinations of multiple experiences displayed in a notary profile:

- Full-Time mobile notary and loan signing agent + freelance job (like website development and graphic design)

- Three or more freelance gigs, like wedding officiant, field inspector, + mobile notary and loan signing agent

- Part-Time mobile notary + temporary contract job or work

- Full time mobile notary + occasional (or regular) contract job or work

- Mobile notary and loan signing agent + Signing company owner + Mentor or trainer

Portfolio Career Example: Bill Soroka

Bill has shared his story of serial entrepreneurship many times. He is an example of what a "portfolio career" may look like. His attraction to the notary business is, in many ways, based on how diverse and flexible this business can be for people that are multi-passionate. Bill refers to this as the "Notary Umbrella."

Bedrock: Experience and Education

Under your notary umbrella, you can provide many other services that both keep you active and engaged in your business AND serve your clients more. As the business owner, it will be your responsibility to use your "About" and "Experience" sections to weave the story that ties all of these interests and services together for your potential customers.

Having multiple businesses within your notary business is quite common these days, and in some ways, it is highly recommended. The key to building wealth and sustainability is having multiple streams of revenue. Below, you'll find some of the most common "side hustles" or revenue sources within a notary business.

Notary +:

- Real Estate Agent
- Website Designer
- Wedding Officiant
- Process Server
- Fingerprint Technician
- Mentor/Trainer
- Tax Preparer
- Legal Document Preparer
- Travel Agent
- Insurance Sales
- Concierge
- Virtual Assistant
- Mortgage Loan Officer

You can position your multiple services under distinct Experience sections and still use the same company listing. LinkedIn will *nest* them together in that instance. You can also describe all of your business services within one Experience description. The choice is yours.

SUPERCHARGER TIP

According to LinkedIn, if your positions are kept up to date, your profile is eighteen times more likely to be found.

Is This You?

If you're starting as a notary . . .	Include your new notary work as a current experience and also your previous jobs as past experiences
If you're working two or three gigs . . .	Create two or three experience sections. Select the one with priority to display first.
If you're working an FT job and notary business on the side . . .	Create two unique work experience sections and decide which one takes priority so you can display that one on top.

SUPERCHARGER TIP

The Work Experience section is strictly about your work experience, while your About essay is more strategic and typically about you in general.

Finally, watch the little details like spelling, grammar, and punctuation. Make sure your previous positions are written in the past tense. Your current experience should be written in the present tense. Stay away from saying you are "responsible for this" and "responsible for that." Instead, use action-oriented verbs and language that is more powerful. Refer to the action verb list we shared in the previous chapter. We also recommend using the first person in this section to make it more interesting and personal.

Education Section

The Education section is so vital to LinkedIn that it's a required element of a complete profile. Be sure to list the school accurately and use the drop-down list so that you can display the university logo. Don't forget to add the exact degree and major for each college. There is also space to provide a bit of information about your activities.

And if you do not have a college degree, don't sweat it. That's one of the beautiful attributes of this business—a college or university degree is not necessary to succeed.

Multiple Colleges and Universities

We recommend you show all the higher education institutions that you attended. There may be notable exceptions, but this is the general rule or best practice. LinkedIn also allows you to rearrange the order of your schools very easily.

SUPERCHARGER TIP

The school shown at the top of your education profile section will automatically display at the very top of your profile.

High School

Many of us have significant friendships and connections from high school, so it is often a good idea to include this for networking reasons. We recommend including your high school. This is often a nice connection to your network. Notary businesses tend to be local, so imagine the possibilities! And why not add your yearbook club, lacrosse team, or other activities?

SUPERCHARGER TIP

Reserve the Education section for your traditional higher education and high school experiences only. Courses, certification programs, leadership programs, and executive education are usually best recorded in the Courses section described in Chapter 7.

CHAPTER 5

FIRST IMPRESSIONS: HEADLINE, PHOTO, AND BANNER

LinkedIn Professional Headline

Your headline should attract prospects and shape opinions! It is such a powerful way to demonstrate your brand and capabilities.

The headline is compelling for two reasons. First, it is significant from a search perspective. The keywords that you select for your headline could be the very words that help a client, prospect, or employer find you.

Secondly, and just as importantly, the headline creates an immediate first impression of you. The viewer sees your partial profile (headshot and headline) and subsequently makes a split-second decision about whether to look at your profile or skip to the next, more exciting person.

You want your headline to be interesting, compelling, and authentic.

You choose the words for your LinkedIn headline, and they will appear near your headshot at the top. Many people don't realize that there is a default setting within LinkedIn. Your latest title from the Experience section is the automatic default headline if you make no adjustments to the settings.

The headline space is very generous from a character count perspective. For several years, we have enjoyed 120 characters. Now we have over 200 characters in this field. This is not to say that you will use all of those characters, but we have much greater flexibility.

Here are some examples of notary headlines. Note that they are all a bit different. You can create the headline that appeals to you. These examples all use keywords and help the prospect understand immediately how the notary can help them!

Lisa Piwcio · 1st
Mobile Notary | Professional Notary Signing Agent

Valerie Dennis · 1st
Notary | Online Notary | Process Server | Mentor

Kevin W. Byrd · 1st
Mobile Notary Public, Certified Signing Agent, Apostille, Friendly Service, Your Place Or

Top Three Headline Creation Tips for Notaries

1. Be strategic and focus on your top priorities. Keep your headline and *About section* in alignment with and complementary to each other. Make sure your headline accurately reflects your personal brand and professional priorities.

2. Be specific with keywords. This will help draw more favorable attention to your expertise. Consider adding words to differentiate yourself from all the other notaries.

3. Consider adding in a little benefit or value statement in your LinkedIn headline. You can add this after keywords or in place of them.

Examples for Notaries

Old headline	Notary Public
New headline	Mobile Notary Serving Lincoln County
Old headline	Notary
New headline	Mobile Notary and Loan Signing Agent | I will come to you!
Old headline	Notary Public
New headline	Notary Public | Certified Loan Signing Agent | Suffolk County and Boston – I will come to your office!
Old headline	Notary Public
New headline	Notary | Reverse Mortgage Specialist | Providing Reliable Signing Services

Examples of Notaries with Two Gigs

Old headline	Notary and Officiant
New headline	Mobile Notary | Dynamic Wedding Officiant | Orlando Area | Full service on your best days…and your worst.

Your headline choice says a lot about you and your brand. Whatever your situation, take your time to think about the best headline for you to attract clients. What would work best with your work and geography?

Headshot Photo

Let's talk about your headshot, which is an *essential* part of your profile. Your prospects and clients want to find, retain, refer, or hire someone who looks professional and polished. As a mobile notary and loan signing agent, we are often hired as a representative of another company or person, and we are sent to the homes and businesses of their clients. The people that hire us want to be sure we represent *their* brand well. Therefore, a headshot is a necessity. Make sure you are smiling and dressed to impress.

Please do not fall into the belief that you will be the exception to this rule. Even if you've been able to rustle up some business without a headshot up to this point, you can trust that your lack of a profile picture (on LinkedIn or any profile) has cost you business and brand reputation. Bill owns a signing company responsible for sending mobile notaries and loan signing agents on assignment in all fifty states, and as he searches for qualified agents, he skips right over *every* profile that does not have a headshot. That lack of a profile picture is an automatic disqualifier.

Many photos have become more casual lately, but select your optimum attire based on the clients you are seeking. If you can afford a professional pho-tographer, it is usually the best investment you can make in your brand and self-confidence. Here are Sandra and Bill's headshots as examples:

SUPERCHARGER TIP

Get a headshot that you love. You will feel more confident online.

Background Banner Images for Notaries

We love background banners! What a fantastic way to represent yourself visually.

Your background banner should reflect your brand. The banner helps reinforce your unique value as a notary and business professional. Many options work well for notaries, including the following:

- Custom banner to match your website and logo
- Image of you at a closing
- Photo of your workplace
- Image of documents with a pen
- Picture of your notary team
- Word cloud about you or your services
- Image montage of your customers
- Photo of you at a trade event
- City skyline
- Harbor view of your city
- Map of your region
- Image of your town square or city landmark
- Call-to-action banner

Here's Bill's banner, which is a call-to-action style.

Bill Soroka · 1st   NotaryCoach.com

Author, Sign & Thrive: How to Make Six Figures as a Mobile Notary and Loan Signing Agent | Founder, NotaryCoach.com | Investor

Greater Phoenix Area · 500+ connections · Contact info

And here's Victoria's example.

Victoria E. Watts · 1st

Signing Agent & Mobile Notary Public

Riverside, California · 42 connections · Contact info

Images

Your banner images should be appropriately sized according to LinkedIn's specifications. Note that the display area for the LinkedIn banner is extremely limited because your headshot and LinkedIn ads can obscure some of the lower parts of the banner.

Be sure to display images with proper permission. Don't just grab an image from a website or Google. Here are several excellent options:

• Photos you have taken yourself (high resolution)

• Images you have personally designed

• Images that you own or have purchased

• Free images from online sites, such as Pixabay, Pexels, or Unsplash

For *free* images, look for those that are clearly labeled as *available for commercial use* and are *attribution free*. This means that you can use them however you wish, but never claim them as your own.

Your LinkedIn background banner should match your personal and company brand. Be consistent between all the words and images on your profile for the best effect. The banner can be a valuable visual expression of your brand.

Canva offers both a free and premium version of their graphic creation portal and smartphone app. This program is great for creating professional grade images for banners, advertising, and social media campaigns. On the resources webpage for this book, you'll find a link to a free course on how to get started with Canva.

Here are some samples of banners we created for the *LinkedIn Club*. Banners are uploaded to position behind a personal headshot. You can make your own banner using Canva or other similar applications. If you choose to use logos from outside organizations or associations, be sure you do so following their guidelines and permissions.

CHAPTER 6

ABOUT SECTION: TELL YOUR STORY

Your LinkedIn essay is a valuable digital real estate. You are now allotted up to 2600 characters to tell the right story to help you attract the perfect client or job. Be sure not to just rehash what is already in your profile, such as where you work or went to school.

Take the time to craft an excellent introduction essay (About). You can genuinely distinguish yourself with an interesting story. You may want to write it in Word or Pages first so you can do a spelling and grammar check before uploading it.

Try to weave together your story in an exciting way to compel your audience to be motivated to work with you or refer you to someone else. This is especially important to do if you have a disjointed work history, or if you offer multiple services under your "notary umbrella."

Consider your viewers

Your preferred viewer will be a prospect for your notary business. The About section is a chance to impress them with how you will help them. You are writing to interest them in your business. What will make the reader want to read all of your profile and contact you for more? Also, your friends, neighbors, volunteering pals, and community connections will also read your page and refer you as a result of what they see.

Use the space

There are now up to 2600 characters available. Don't give up because it's hard to write about yourself. This space is a golden opportunity for the pre-selling of your personal brand. LinkedIn reported that an essay of at least forty words makes your profile more likely to be found in search. Most of Sandra's clients include two or three paragraphs of content in their essay.

LinkedIn allows for the most generous space and character use. Spend some time here and really create awesome material that you can use to seed all the other online profiles a notary should have optimized.

Directories you can fill with your LinkedIn profile data:

- www.signingagent.com

- www.notarycafe.com

- www.notaryrotary.com

- www.123notary.com

- www.reversenotary.com

- Practically ANY online directory or profile listing!

Be Real, Genuine, and Personal

It should reflect the real you as a worker, leader, notary, volunteer, and so on. Consider including a brief mention of your personal interests somewhere in your essay.

Make it compelling by using the first-person tense. This creates warmth for your reader.

Remember the four pillars we discussed earlier? Bring them through in your About section. People work with who they know, like, and trust. Use your About essay to give your audience the chance to get to know you a bit. Demonstrate your competence, confidence, and integrity with keywords that are relevant to their needs.

And don't forget about *passion*. Do you love what you do and who you do it for? Let that come through in your essay/summary. Your enthusiasm is contagious. Your mobile notary and loan signing business is about far more than just signing, dating, and stamping paper. Let your readers feel that in your words.

Consider language

Use the words that you wish to be known and found for in your About section. Make sure it all sounds natural and authentic. At the end of your essay, you may want to list out the specialties or focus areas in a list. This creates a nice visual. Some of your readers will prefer to read a list, and it is a chance to repeat your keywords.

Start strong with a hook

Start with an interesting hook for an opening sentence and paragraph. This may be a question or an authentic opening. Draw your reader in with your own story at the beginning of your About section. Your goal is to motivate your profile visitor to click on *see more* to continue reading.

Is this YOU?

Persona	About ideas
Problem solver	Your approach, what problems you solve, how you are most helpful to clients, why people hire you.
Visionary	What inspires you, your vision for the world, community, or industry; your unique perspective.
New Notary	Your enthusiasm for the notary role, what unique value you will bring from your past experiences.
Multiple Gigs	Explain your multiple gigs and try to weave in an overarching theme, which may be personal values or expertise.

SUPERCHARGER TIP

Think of your About section as an introduction opportunity!

Need a structure? Consider this 5 H format developed by Sandra:

Hook – Start with a compelling opening. Do you have a story about how you got into the notary business or why you do this work?

Help – Describe how you help your clients. Focus on their success.

Human – Add some personality, passion, or personal interests. People hire people!

Hot-words – Incorporate keywords and notary language naturally.

Hello – Add your contact information at the end.

Possible Ideas for Your Notary Essay

Consider trying to answer one of these questions that may be very interesting for your About section:

- Why I became a notary?

- How I solve client problems?

- Why people hire me?

- My clients are . . .?

- How I got interested in the notary world?

- How I manage notary and X together? (This approach is great for a port-folio career)

- Why I love doing this...?

SUPERCHARGER TIP

Consider using your About section to describe what you are grateful for!

How to add the Human H?

People buy and hire people they like and admire. Find a way to introduce the human element into your essay. Here are a few ways to do that:

- Tell your story by explaining what drew you to the notary business or how you started

- Add your personal interests as the last paragraph in your essay, such as "When I am not working, I enjoy hiking, tennis, and spending time with my family."

- Weave in your interests by comparing them to your business or ap-proach

- Include your unique insights and tie them back to something personal

LinkedIn About Section: Format, Spacing, Emojis, and Appearance

Make sure your essay looks as great as it sounds. Consider using capital letters to differentiate different headings. Consider symbols and emojis but use them sparingly. LinkedIn's current editing options are limited. You will want some white space to improve the overall appearance.

Use an Attractive Layout

Make sure your essay has an appealing layout. You are somewhat limited by LinkedIn's editing features in this section, but you can use spacing, capitalization, and symbols in your profile to make it more attractive. For example, you can capitalize on a paragraph heading to make it stand out more prominently.

Strong Ending

At the end of your About section, consider listing your *specialties* (unless you are an attorney), some personal interests, and your contact information. There are a few reasons to do this:

1. The focus list is an opportunity to use your keywords and add to the essay's visual appeal.

2. Personal interests can draw people to you. We buy from and hire people who we like. We all look for things we have in common. For that reason, Sandra includes her interests in skiing, walking, and history near the bottom of her essay.

3. You want to be very easy to contact. Include your contact information at the bottom of your essay. Make it as easy as possible to be contacted. Even though you have your contact info in the designated areas on LinkedIn, include it here in your About essay. If people have to hit back buttons or navigate to other screens, you'll lose them.

CASE STUDY EXAMPLE 1:

About Essay by Lorraine Schechter from Bend, Oregon

Being a mobile Notary Public is the perfect career for me. I am passionate about helping people achieve their goals and dreams! As a mobile notary, it is always a wonderful surprise as to whom I get to meet and where (a goat pen at the County Fairgrounds is still top of my list). Each day and each meeting are a new adventure.

As Notaries Public, we have the opportunity to enrich the lives of others. We play an important role in their life-changing decisions. Being mobile, I also provide a convenient service to others. Far beyond a notarial signature and seal, I enjoy celebrating the good times and have compassion during life's more challenging situations.

MY OFFER TO YOU:

My background and continuing education have prepared me to assist my clients in even the most complicated of situations. My knowledge and skills provide expertise to address potential issues before the appointment.

Above and beyond, I go the distance to ensure that the signing experience is accurate as well as pleasant. For good measure, I triple-check my work and return documents quickly. I use secure systems to safeguard the privacy of your clients' personal information.

Transparency through communication with your signers and appropriate parties (signing companies, loan officers, escrow officers, and attorneys) is of utmost importance to me to ensure a smooth signing process. In addition to serving many individuals, I have had the privilege of working with companies such as Western Title & Escrow, AmeriTitle, Deschutes County Title Company, First American Title Insurance Company, WFG Lender Services, Title 365, BankServ Nationwide Notary Service, and many more. I am accountable for my work. On the rare occasion of an error, I fix it - fast.

My goal is to be a part of your team, assisting you and providing you with peace of mind.

DOCUMENT SPECIALTIES INCLUDE:

○ Loan Documents: Reverse Mortgages, 1st & 2nd Purchase, Refinance Loans, VA & FHA, Construction

○ Manufactured Home, REOs, HELOCs

○ Loan Applications

○ Estate Documents - Trusts and Wills

ADDITIONAL SERVICES:

○ Form I-9 Verification

○ Field Service Inspections

A LITTLE ABOUT ME:

When not working, I enjoy volunteering for community projects, numerous outdoor activities in beautiful Central Oregon, organic gardening & cooking, and learning Qigong.

Fast. Efficient. Mobile.

Contact me for a free consultation at:

✉ acceleratednotary@gmail.com

☎541-771-1937

☞ www.acceleratednotary.com

CASE STUDY EXAMPLE 2:

About essay by Kevin Byrd of Stockton, California

Kevin writes a shorter essay. Even though it doesn't follow the exact format we typically suggest, we like it because it clearly explains how he helps clients while being personal and friendly. We loved reading about his wife and Dad as much as we enjoyed reading about his unique clients.

I provide professional, courteous and reliable Mobile Notary Service, Electronic Notary services via DocVerify's E-Signature platform, Apostille services, and loan document signing services in San Joaquin County, for all your Document and Loan Signing needs. I also service the country jail and area prisons as well as hospitals and convalescent homes.

I take pride in service your clients, assisting them in completing their documents in accordance with all state laws. I've completed several thousand load signings in the last 16 years including commercial, hard money loas, reverse mortgages, sales and refinance mortgages. I'm available before and after business hours and weekends when I'm not with the family on the delta, or at some RV park with my wife of 39 years and my 96-year-old- father who still loves to get out and fish, and enjoy the outdoors whenever I say let's go.

Your About, Headline, and Experience:

The About, headline, and experience sections all work together along with the other part of your profile. Together they paint the complete picture of you and your brand. Review them separately and then also as a complete picture.

SUPERCHARGER TIP

Your essay is a golden opportunity to position yourself and create a wonderful impression!

CHAPTER 7

BE DISTINCTIVE: SPECIAL PROFILE SECTIONS

LinkedIn offers many other special profile sections that are wonderful for notaries. These are optional sections that you are able to add at any time.

Courses

You may list relevant courses in the *Courses* section of the LinkedIn profile.
This is an immensely powerful way to highlight the notary and business clas-
ses you have taken. It is not necessary to list all of your college courses, but
consider adding those that are unique or related to your current or future
work.

Example Courses:

- Your State Required Notary Training (if applicable)

- The Sign & Thrive Notary Training Course and Community

- The Notary Institute's Apostille Training Course

- The NNA Immigrations Form Specialist Course

- The Laura Biewer Presents...Training and Replay Library

- Notary2Pro

- LinkedIn for Personal Best Club

- Six Sigma

- What other professional or even personal courses have you taken throughout your career?

Licenses and Certifications

Use the *Licenses and Certification* section for your designations, certifications, and licenses.

Under the Licenses and Certifications section on LinkedIn, you will be listing the name of the certification, the certifying authority, license number, the certification URL, and the applicable dates. In some cases, the license number is not necessary for your profile, but the name and certifying authority are essential.

Be sure to add your relevant certifications such as:

- Certified Notary Signing Agent (NSA) from National Notary Association

- Certified Reverse Mortgage Signing Professional (CRMSP) from Notary Coach

- Loan Signing Agent Certification from Notary2Pro.com

Certified Signing Agent by National Notary Association
National Notary Association
See credential

Rearrange the order of your certifications so your most strategic ones are on top. At some point, you may choose to delete old and irrelevant certifications.

Test Scores and GPA

Test scores or GPAs are generally not relevant for professionals on LinkedIn. This is especially true of a mature worker who has been out of college for several years. Your SAT, GRE, or GMAT score is just too much information for most of us.

Organizations

The Organizations section is an opportunity to highlight the professional associations and organizations that you're involved with. This may include:

- National Notary Association (NNA);

- Notary Association for Your State

- American Society of Notaries

- American Land Title Association (ALTA)

- California League of Independent Notaries (CLIN)—If you're in California, be sure to get dialed in with this advocacy group.

Perhaps you belong to local business or civic groups, such as the Chamber of Commerce, Rotary Club, or BNI (Business Networking International).

Display your affiliations in the Organization section of your profile. Enter the name of the organization, your position, dates, and a brief description. Be sure to use the drop-down menu and select the company or university that you worked for while a member of the organization so that the organization links to that position on your profile.

Later on, as we discuss researching and connecting with your ideal customers, you'll see that this section on organizations comes in handy when you're looking for a unique and creative way to reach out.

Publications

Are you a writer? The Publications section is one of our favorites because there are so many ways to use it to share your expertise and brand. Publications by or about you instill trust, credibility, and confidence.

Enter the title, publisher, description, publication dates, and any co-authors. Add a URL if the article or book is online. This section may be used for:

- Articles or blogs authored by you. If you are a prolific article writer or blogger, select the most strategic ones to highlight on your LinkedIn profile.

- Articles written about you or quoting or mentioning you. Add the title, date, and a short description. Always be clear and add the name of the article author; otherwise, it's assumed that you wrote the piece. Link to the author's profile. You may decide to add your quote or explain that you were mentioned in the article.

- Your book or e-book. Indicate the date and publisher and add a description. Use the link to connect to the e-commerce site for the purchase of your text, such as the Amazon page.

Languages

Some of your prospects will be seeking notary support in various languages. Add the languages that you speak and the level of proficiency in your LinkedIn profile under *Accomplishments*. However, if you only speak one language such as English, we recommend that you do not indicate that as your language since it is implied. If you are multilingual, you may want to consider creating a second version of your profile with your second or third language.

Volunteering

Are you a volunteer?

SUPERCHARGER TIP

Volunteering in your community is an excellent way to become known and enhance the trust factor beyond your immediate network.

Prospective clients and business partners place value in volunteering activities. In the Volunteering section of LinkedIn (part of the Background section), list the organization name, your role, date, and a brief description. When you enter the organization's name, you'll have the opportunity to add the logo to your profile by selecting the proper drop-down choice.

The volunteer work you do can often be a valuable reflection of your personal brand.

Example: Bill's Volunteering section

Volunteer Experience

Volunteer
RELEASE THE FEAR
Children

Release the Fear is an incredible organization that helps youth transcend violence through the creative process. I've helped facilitate workshops, market events, write grants, raise money, and more.

Fundraising Chair
One Voice Community Center
Civil Rights and Social Action

This was a board position where I created and coordinated various fundraising events to support the Center.

Honors and Awards

Take the opportunity to highlight your awards and any special recognition. Industry awards are appropriate for this section. This could include credit for a "top notary" in your city or county or a "Voted Best Notary in _____ County Two Years in a Row!" type of award.

Add awards you received while attending a college or university. This may include Phi Beta Kappa, cum laude, summa cum laude, magna cum laude, valedictorian, or special awards unique to your school or department.

This is also a great spot if you've received any kind of community recognition. One of Sandra's clients received the award called *40 under 40*, which was an excellent addition to her LinkedIn profile awards section.

Award Examples:

- NNA Notary of the Year Award

- Distinguished Speaker Awards

- Best Notary in your County

Projects

You can be extremely creative in how you use the Projects section. You might want to use the Projects section to list various projects or programs that are outside of your everyday business responsibilities. Perhaps you were involved in a particular program with the National Notary Association or a community organization? Consider using the Project section to highlight those types of activities.

Here's what to include in the Projects section: the project name, date, team members, and description. Be sure to link it to your occupation with the drop-down menu. The other great thing about the Projects section is that you can add a URL and link to a webpage. Include other team members for your projects. Remember to link to your Experience or Education sections using the drop-down menu.

Always think of your personal brand when it comes to deciding which projects to highlight. If they are outside of your brand mission, just leave them off. Feel free to continually add, delete, and prioritize the projects in your profile.

CHAPTER 8

SOCIAL PROOF: RECOMMENDATIONS, SKILLS, AND ENDORSEMENTS

Today's notary businesses often rely on online reviews. Your clients may be writing about you on Google, Yelp, or Facebook. LinkedIn also offers a wonderful opportunity for testimonials. As part of a thoughtful business community, we should be giving reviews as well as requesting them.

Peer validation (or social proof) on LinkedIn can make the difference of you being found, hired, and trusted. It takes effort. The people in your network that have LinkedIn recommendations and endorsements on their profiles have worked at it. This online peer validation generally doesn't materialize on your profile without some effort and attention from you.

Accentuate Your Top Skills

The first thing you need to do is select the most strategic skills so you will be found and endorsed for the things that matter to your ideal clients.

Remove any skills that do not apply to you. You don't want words listed that are not a match for you and your business. Just because someone has endorsed you for a skill, this does not mean it is right for your profile and personal brand.

Make sure you have your most strategic skills at the top of your list. The top three skills listed on your profile should be the most relevant ones that complement your brand. Within the skills editing section, you need to *pin* the top skills so that they will position at the top of your profile.

Your skills list is likely to change over time, so check this every few months and rearrange. LinkedIn allows you to move them around (drag) so you can easily prioritize them for your profile viewers.

Excellent skills for Notaries include:

- Notary Public

- Loan Signing

- Organizational

- Communication

- Attention to Detail

- Mobile and Convenient

- Logistically Astute

- Punctual

- Customer Service

- Notary Law

- Critical Thinking

- Notary Solutions

- Committed to Win-Win Relationships

Here is an example of Lorraine Schechter's skills and endorsements on LinkedIn.

Skills & Endorsements

✓ **Notary Public** · 2

You and 1 connection have given endorsements for this skill

✓ **Certified Notary Signing Agent.** · 2

You and 1 connection have given endorsements for this skill

✓ **Estate/Trust Signing Agent** · 1

You have endorsed Lorraine for this skill

SUPERCHARGER TIP

We recommend displaying your industry skills on the top of your skill list, but remember to include soft skills too.

Endorsements

Endorsements are an easy way to provide positive recognition to a first-level connection. It's a friendly and helpful gesture you can make for your contact.

Start by endorsing others often. Make it a routine, but always do it authentically. Endorse coworkers, customers, vendors, referral partners, other notaries, or anyone who has helped you, has taught you something, or has skills you can authentically vouch for.

Timing is key. Endorse someone the day he or she helped you solve a problem or the day he or she taught you a new skill. Endorse someone after a great meeting, class, or after receiving advice or a favor. Endorse people for skills that you know they possess.

It's smart to ask for endorsements from your referral partners and possibly clients too. Let them know you have rearranged and prioritized your skills on your LinkedIn profile. Just ask. Of course, it's always lovely to endorse them first and discuss the skills that you both have—and skills that you are developing. It usually leads to a friendly conversation about personal development and learning.

Endorsements are a form of gratitude. Consider creating time on your calendar to really check in with who has helped you this week. Think of "Endorsement Thursdays" or whatever works for your schedule.

SUPERCHARGER TIP

Only endorse people that you know and do so authentically for the skills they possess!

Recommendations

LinkedIn recommendations are pure gold. They provide valuable social proof to your network. Your first-level connections personally write recommendations. You approve the content before it displays on your profile. It takes more time and thought than an endorsement.

SUPERCHARGER TIP

Try to get at least three recommendations. Be sure to give them also!

You approve and manage the display of each written recommendation on your LinkedIn profile. A LinkedIn recommendation is a public online validation of your work and capabilities.

To get the written recommendations, you will need to ask clients, partners, referral sources, employers, and community connections. The best time to ask for a recommendation is when you are concluding a project, assignment, or job.

Getting Recommendations the Right Way

Here is our step-by-step process of asking for a recommendation:

1. Decide who in your network can best describe your work firsthand as a result of your work together. Make a list of possible people to ask.

2. Always consider the timing for the best results. The best time may be just as you are finishing a project or a job with a client. Always remember to ask as you are leaving one job or project for another. Ask as soon as your client gives you a big compliment.

3. Ask for the recommendation. If it's someone very close, you can send him or her a note or LinkedIn recommendation request. If it's someone you haven't talked to in a while, we recommend you warm him or her up a bit. Give him or her a call or meet for coffee. Tell him or her how vital project X was and that you are working on your LinkedIn profile. Let him or her know that this recommendation is crucial to you and appreciated. Make a personalized request to dramatically increase your success rate.

4. Once he or she agrees, ask how you can make it easy. Would he or she like some ideas about what to say? Or perhaps you offer to draft or to edit? Send him or her the link directly from LinkedIn.

5. You may need to follow up with your colleague. People often have the very best intentions but fail to complete a task. A gentle reminder is smart. Your connection may be confused about how to do it, so you may have to provide some navigational guidance.

6. Show gratitude. Send your friend, manager, or customer a thank you note or LinkedIn message for their thoughtful recommendation.

SUPERCHARGER TIP

Consider the people who hire you or refer you regularly as a candidate to write a LinkedIn recommendation for your profile!

It's perfectly OK to recommend someone who recommends you. This fact is especially relevant for team situations or referral partners. Why not initiate a conversation such as this after a project: "I enjoyed working with you. We had the best team! I am very proud of our results. Let's write a LinkedIn recommendation for each other based on this great achievement."

Giving Recommendations and Endorsements

Writing recommendations for others is as valuable as receiving them yourself. For leaders, they are even more critical. Be sure to be generous by giving authentic recommendations to people who have worked for you as an employee, partner, or vendor. Well-written specific recommendations reflect positively on the writer and the recipient.

Giving recommendations and endorsements is just as important as getting them! There are so many reasons. Here are a few of my favorites:

- It's the right thing to do! If you appreciate someone's work, then support him or her with an endorsement or recommendation. Simple.

- You are a leader or mentor. You encourage, support, and help others as a leader. If you notice a leader who doesn't give recommendations, it just doesn't look right. This issue is magnified for a leader who has received but not given recommendations.

- You will be noticed on the page of the person you are recommending. Your profile will be visible on the page of the superstar you endorsed or recommended.

- Giving often prompts getting. And that is OK as long as the endorsements and recommendations are meaningful and genuine.

How to Give Recommendations

The mechanics are simple. Go directly to your colleague's profile to recommend him or her. However, it usually makes sense to discuss the recommendation first. Make sure you are mentioning what is most important—and usually, he or she can guide you a little bit.

Your colleagues, clients, and vendors will be delighted if you give them a genuine endorsement or recommendation. Figure out which one is most suitable for the situation. Your vendors, colleagues, and team will appreciate a written recommendation, but it might not be ideal for your customer or manager. Use an endorsement for that situation. There's no reason not to endorse a customer or manager as long as it's authentic.

The best written recommendations are specific and timely. Saying "She's a true professional" is usually not as meaningful as describing a particular situation with details.

SUPERCHARGER TIP

You manage your recommendations. You choose which ones to accept and display.

Received (2)   Given (3)

"Genuine Expert" is the phrase that comes to mind when I think about Lorraine and her Accelerated Notary business. She has exceptional skills as a mobile Notary Public top professional in the greater Bend, OR region. She is very adept in working with individuals and businesses to help navigate a variety of life circumstances as an well-experienced, certified signing agent. Lorraine will walk her clients through all aspects of the notarizing process step-by-step. Her enthusiasm and dedication is both inspiring and motivating to all her clients, customers and colleagues. Lorraine earns my highest recommendation! See less

Social Proof: Recommendations, Skills, and Endorsements

Your recommendations and endorsements will reflect directly on your brand and network. They are the best forms of social proof. Spend the time to work on these to benefit your network and yourself.

CHAPTER 9

ROUND-UP AND SIZZLE TIME

You are now ready to think about the final touches—and maybe add some extra Sizzle—to your LinkedIn profile. Simply uploading text and images is not enough. You want to make your profile meaningful and attractive. And you want it to be working for you! There are several ways to do this.

Brand Clarity

If you are displaying too many different and unrelated skills and experiences, your brand will be confusing. Too much information can sometimes hurt your positioning. Remove anything irrelevant to your brand and priorities. The same can be said for status updates. Keep the majority of your updates and likes centered on your brand and those that support your network.

Technical Accuracy and Consistency

Your profile would be your responsibility, even if you hired someone to help you write your profile or résumé. You are the one who will approve all content. There are several ways to check it:

- Make sure your profile dates are consistent with your résumé. If you are in a job search, be aware that some recruiters will immediately disregard a candidate with varying dates.

- Use the same type of bullet point (or colon or dash) throughout.

- Be consistent with how you start and end sentences that are part of a list. For example, start them all with a present or past action verb and complete them all with a period (or not).

- Remove anything that is not 100 percent true. Enough said.

- Check the language throughout. Be consistent with tenses. Don't mix the third person and the first person tense in your profile.

- Run your About essay and Experience descriptions through grammar and spelling software before posting.

- Check the general readability of your sections.

- Have a good friend do a read-through for an accuracy check. He or she might see something that you miss.

Duplicate Profiles

Search for your name on LinkedIn to make sure there aren't any duplicate profiles on display. You don't want people finding that old profile you haven't updated in five years.

Format and Appearance

Some of the sections are lengthy, particularly the About essay and Experience sections. Consider the overall appearance and readability. The following are examples of what to avoid:

- one enormous paragraph with no breaks or bullets

- too many bullet points

- no white space

- unattractive spacing

LinkedIn does not allow for bold, italics, or underlining, so make fair use of white space, bullets, and capital letters.

Symbols, Emojis, and Capital Letters

🔥 Sizzle Alert

It's nice to see an essay or post that is very attractively laid out with clearly differentiated sections. If you have two or three distinct topics or themes in your profile, consider using capital letters as a heading. Don't use all caps throughout because they are symbolic of shouting online.

For your bullet points, consider using symbols or emojis to make the topics more exciting and distinct. Here are some examples:

For bullets, you can use the following:

► ► ◙ ❖ ⌨ ★ ✔ ✗

Other symbols you can use for phone and email are as follows:

✆ ☎ ☏ ✉

Find your symbols and emojis. Apply them directly or copy and paste them over to LinkedIn.

SUPERCHARGER TIP

Use symbols and emojis for emphasis. Try not to go overboard. Use them sparingly.

Separators for Your Headline

Use a comma or the vertical pipeline separator (sometimes called a pipe or vertical pipeline) symbol to separate phrases in a headline. On many keyboards, this is located above the return key on the same key as the backslash.

\ for the backslash

Shift + | for the pipe separator

Unlock the "Open to Work" Feature

 Sizzle Alert

This feature is designed for job seekers, but there's no reason you can't use it for your benefit. Companies who wish to hire notaries can find you to fill their *job,* which might be full-time, contract, part-time, or freelancer. Use this feature so you will show up in job searches!

You have the option of sharing your career and geographic interests on your LinkedIn profile. The best part is that you control the visibility. Your options are to show this information to recruiters only or to everyone. Read the options and decide which option will be best for you. This feature was designed for job seekers, but it might work well for you if you wish to be hired by a company on a contract basis.

Consider Trying LinkedIn's ProFinder Service

🔥 Sizzle Alert

LinkedIn now offers *ProFinder*, a professional services marketplace in the USA, for specific service categories, but we expect to see it expanded in the future. Fortunately, the notary service is one of the available service types! There is no financial compensation paid to LinkedIn, so the service is entirely free for you.

A LinkedIn member can request a proposal for one of the selected services on the list and then receive five proposals within 24 hours. This image below is the beginning of the process for the customer. After completing this, the next questions are about types of service, timing, scope, additional details, and location.

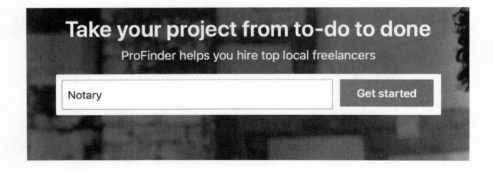

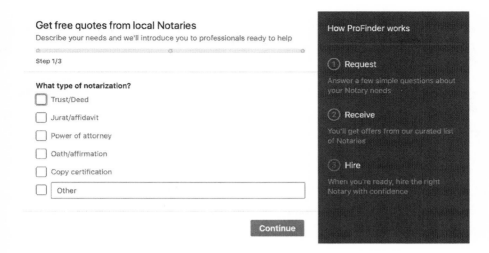

You will need to apply to participate. LinkedIn pulls your profile content directly to create a unique ProFinder page. Prospective clients will be viewing the ProFinder version of your LinkedIn profile. LinkedIn recommendations are essential for ProFinder. Overall, this feature works well for some professions, but the key is to be organized and quickly send off a great proposal or offer. Besides, your outstanding profile is key to winning these fast deals!

Open For Business Feature for Notaries

🔥 Sizzle Alert

The *Open for Business* feature allows you to be found by people searching for notary services. It is promising but not fully rolled out or available yet (as of this writing). Currently, service providers can sign up for a waitlist for this capability. Hopefully, this situation will change by the time you read this book. The benefits of *Open for Business* are the following: LinkedIn members can easily find you via search filters, and then they can message you about your notary services for free.

Check Out Your Profile on Your Mobile Devices

Be sure to check how your profile renders on your tablet and mobile devices. You might want to adjust things accordingly.

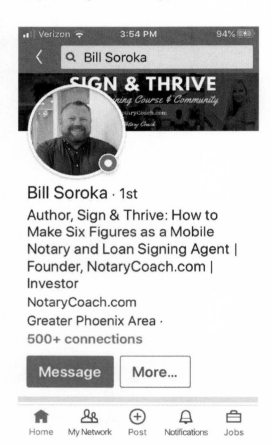

Your Introduction Card

The top of your profile is called the *Introduction card*. People may form an immediate impression of you here. Double-check to make sure this is in perfect order. Here is Sandra's introduction card:

Twitter Link

🔥 Sizzle Alert

Consider connecting your Twitter account to LinkedIn. This setting will allow you to post simultaneously to both Twitter and LinkedIn.

Web Links

Your LinkedIn profile offers many opportunities to include your website and landing page links in the Contact Info, Featured, Projects, and Publications sections. Interested parties may click from your profile directly to your site. Double check all your links!

Multilingual? Consider a Profile in a Second or Third Language

LinkedIn supports twenty-four languages. You may easily create a second or third version of your profile in another language. While LinkedIn provides the platform, you need to do the translation and then upload it. Your viewer will be able to see the profile version that matches what they are using on LinkedIn as a primary language.

SUPERCHARGER TIP

If you're multilingual, consider creating a second or third version of LinkedIn for each language you speak.

Religion and Politics

Sandra advises her workshop clients not to post views that pertain to religion and politics. It's undoubtedly essential to list the church, synagogue, government, or political office where you work. It's quite another thing to post extreme religious or political views on your home feed or as a blog post. We have all seen some over-the-top posts that are very controversial. Think before you post, and you should be fine.

Where to Edit? Desktop – Mobile — Tablet

We recommend making LinkedIn profile edits on your desktop or laptop. Yes, you can make some changes on mobile or tablet, but the editing functionality is limited.

Promote Your Profile

Now that your LinkedIn profile is in fabulous shape, have you thought about sharing it? Now is the time to:

- Add the link to notary directory sites where you are listed

- Add the link to your email signature (or create a graphic with an email signature tool)

- Add a link from your website

- Add your LinkedIn profile to other social sites (YouTube, Instagram, Twitter, etc.)

- Add your profile link to any online directories where you are listed

Stay Up to Date

Keep your LinkedIn profile up to date at all times. Don't get into the situation where you lose opportunities!

CHAPTER 10

COMPANY PAGE FOR YOUR NOTARY BUSINESS

Your notary company can have its own distinct page presence on LinkedIn. Companies benefit greatly by having their own (company) page on LinkedIn. There is no charge from LinkedIn to use this basic capability, but you may want to hire a professional to set the page up for your business correctly or get expert instruction.

Page Benefits for Notaries

- A specific web page devoted to your company with a logo, banner, specialties, and SEO-capable description.

- Increased visibility on Google search, LinkedIn search, status updates, and from employee profiles.

- Post and share content. Engage with clients, partners, and prospects.

- Display your logo on your personal profile. This logo is also a direct link to your company's page.

- Gain company followers who will receive your company's status updates in their personal news feeds.

- View and analyze your followers.

- Invite clients and prospects to follow your page.

- Post jobs and attract candidates.

SUPERCHARGER TIP

Make sure your *personal* profile is on-point and you are proud of it before you create a Company Page.

Let's Get Ready to Create a LinkedIn Page for Your Notary Business!

LinkedIn pages are established online by individual users. The starting point is a correctly set up LinkedIn personal profile with either an intermediate or All-Star profile strength. This minimum threshold makes sense. LinkedIn wants legitimate users to be able to create LinkedIn company pages.

Other best practices and requirements include the following:

- Make sure a page doesn't already exist for your organization. You don't want to create a duplicate.

- The person setting up the page (the admin) should have the position and company listed in the Experience section of his profile and a confirmed email address from the company.

- Confirm the email address associated with your account.

Content to Post on Your Company Page

What your company posts online for LinkedIn, Facebook, Twitter, or Instagram has a significant impact on your company brand. Look at Chapter 14 for specific content ideas and tips, which can apply to your personal or company page. Additionally, here is a list of possible content to post on a company page:

- blog articles from company website—with a link

- thought leadership notary content

- tips and ideas that will help a notary client

- notary news and articles

- employee updates

- company news and updates

- upcoming events

- partner or client news

- community initiatives

- customer photo and thank you

SUPERCHARGER TIP

Try to keep at least 80 percent of your content informational and helpful. Less than 20 percent should be about your services.

Increase Your Page Followers

Everyone wants to increase their page follower count. Here are a few ideas:

- Ask employees to link profiles in their Experience section to the company page.

- Add a link or a plug-in to the company website that points to the LinkedIn company page.

- Add a link or a badge to the company page on your email signature—with a request to follow.

- Promote the page on Facebook, Twitter, or Instagram

- Ask or invite your first-level connections to follow the page.

- Add an invitation to follow and a link at the bottom of your blog posts.

- Add an invitation to follow on all written documents.

- Ask partners to follow (start by following their pages).

- Ask customers to follow (start by following their pages).

- Use images and hashtags on posts and ask questions for better engagement.

Finding and Following Other Pages

Find pages by entering the name in the search bar and selecting the drop-down titled *Companies*. You can also click on the logo of the page from the status updates in your news feed or directly from employee profile pages.

Consider following the company pages of your partners, prospects, and clients. Their company content may now appear in your feed.

Notaries can also learn valuable intelligence from a LinkedIn company page. Be the first one to hear about a significant event at your client or prospect's business. Then be the first one to message your prospect with a personally targeted approach.

SUPERCHARGER TIP

LinkedIn Pages are wonderful to establish a larger digital presence and display your brand. We recommend having a page for your business, but your first priority should always be to have a complete and compelling personal profile. The majority of engagement and opportunities will be from your efforts as an individual on LinkedIn.

CHAPTER 11

NETWORKING FOR NOTARY SUCCESS

Notary clients and prospects are using LinkedIn to connect and learn. Your prospects are there, but where are you? Are you connecting and following up? Are you researching your prospects on LinkedIn? Are you engaging with people in your network?

The best way to create a strategic network is to be proactive, helpful, personal, and engaging. Invite and message people with friendly notes. Provide help, recommendations, introductions, and advice. If you sit by the sidelines and wonder why LinkedIn isn't working, it's because you probably need to actively participate to a higher degree. Use LinkedIn for relationship building, sharing expertise, and starting conversations. Be enthusiastically helpful!

Use LinkedIn as a tool to help you build relationships. Once you are active and helpful, you can expect the following to happen as a natural outgrowth:

- Introductions and referrals

- Likes and comments on your posts

- Sales and career opportunities

This topic of LinkedIn proactive networking and community is so essential that Sandra focused her TEDx talk on this very topic. Please check out her 11-minute speech on YouTube called *LinkedIn Community; A Super-Power Hiding in Plain Sight.* We will include the link on the resource page.

LinkedIn Connections

First-level connections are reserved for our most meaningful relationships on LinkedIn. It requires acceptance from both parties, unlike a *follower* relationship. Second-level connections are our *friends of friends* and typically comprise of a vast pool of potential introductions and referrals. Third-level connections are the next step removed from the second-level. You can identify your relationship level by the icon on the person's profile page when you view it from your account.

One of the most critical personal metrics is the number of first-level connections. Your first-level relationships are to be cherished and protected. For most of us, we want to connect with people we know, like, and trust. Accepting strangers into our network might make sense, too, if there is a good reason that aligns with your networking or branding strategy. You decide your network strategy and then invite or accept people accordingly.

SUPERCHARGER TIP

Aim to build a network of 500 or more high-quality connections if you are actively growing your notary business.

You might decide to connect with people in your industry or from your city that you wish to know. We suggest reviewing every profile carefully before deciding to connect. Don't just accept anyone on LinkedIn.

Things to consider when someone invites you to connect include:

- Mutual connections are always good to see because this is someone you are already connected to indirectly.

- A completed LinkedIn profile shows someone who is serious about business. An empty profile with few connections might even be suspicious.

- Location might matter; however, you never know who knows who.

- Things in common: school, past experiences, volunteering, or interests.

Your Followers

Your followers are also part of your overall LinkedIn community. Your first level connections become mutual followers automatically as you connect with them. If you are a content producer, trainer, or influencer, you are likely to get distinct followers who are not officially *connected*. LinkedIn allows you to display a *follow* or *connect* button as a primary *call to action* on your profile. Expect that your followers may be engaging with your content. Check out your followers, and you may be surprised to find some valuable connection-ready people in the ranks.

Build a Strategic Network by Being Pro-Active

We all create our own LinkedIn universe. You invite, select, and approve your first-level connections. Those first-level connections are the foundation of your community because they are typically the best gateway to opportunities, conversation, and new relationships. Beyond that, your LinkedIn network includes second and third-level connections and group members.

The best practice for building a strategic network is to be pro-active with your invitations to connect. Why? Because these are the people who already know you or have some degree of familiarity with you. Even if you are changing careers or pivoting, your first level connections know your work ethic, values, and skills. They like you. They trust you. Be sure to connect with:

- Clients and prospects

- Notary connections

- Referral partners

- Current and past colleagues

- Community and volunteering friends

- Relatives, neighbors, friends, etc.

- Alumni and educational contacts

Consider the following opportunities that can develop from friendly connecting on LinkedIn.

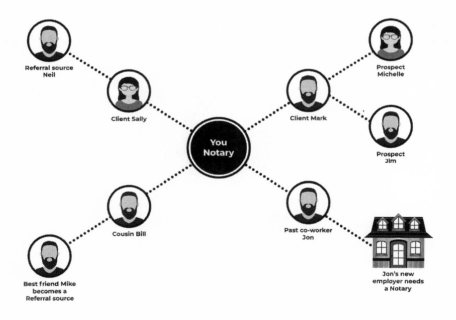

Examples of Fabulous Notary Networking

You meet someone at a networking event and enjoy a nice conversation	Follow-up with a LinkedIn invitation and personal note saying you enjoyed meeting. Find something nice to say about something you saw on their profile.
You meet someone on one of Bill's Zoom meetings within the context of a large group.	Send a LinkedIn invitation mentioning the Zoom meeting. Say you enjoyed the webinar and would be happy to connect.
You do a closing with a new client.	Invite them to connect with a thank you note.
You meet someone in your community for the first time, either in person or online.	Send a friendly invitation to connect. Say you enjoyed meeting them. Ask about them! When you show interest in others, they will likely do the same.
You are part of a training or learning community	Invite fellow community members to connect with a friendly message.

Conferences
Events
Community
Volunteering
Networking
Office Pop-Ins
Closings
Toastmaster

The Relationship Cycle

As you reach out and connect with people on LinkedIn, do it from a place of authentic connection to another human being—not (and I repeat NOT) to sell them something. Sure, they may very well be your ideal customer, and you may really be able to help them or vice-versa, but honor the natural relationship cycle before you go pitching your services.

Start with a simple connection. Send a message that includes a reason you think you'd like to connect (something in common, respect, connections in common, etc.).

Use the strategies in the upcoming chapters to continually add value to the relationship. This will look like commenting on their posts, liking their content, sharing their posts, creating your own relevant content, and even endorsing or recommending (as previously discussed).

As your relationship progresses and you build rapport, you might consider then reaching out through the LinkedIn messenger or even through email to see if this connection is interested in taking the relationship to the next level.

Sometimes the most successful online connections happen the sooner you take them offline, like through a traditional phone call, office meeting, coffee break, happy hour, or, like during the pandemic of 2020, even a Zoom call.

All of this is said to help you avoid the single most common mistake contactors make on LinkedIn, which is to connect with a direct message followed by an immediate pitch. Avoid selling yourself, your services, or your products in the initial connection message or invitation to connect.

It is perceived as tacky and unprofessional, and it just doesn't work. More so than that, it is profoundly disrespectful to the beauty of relationships. You're laying the foundation for one single connection that could quite literally change everything for you and your business. Do everything in your power to honor that. And don't let a slip-up in etiquette at the very beginning of a relationship jeopardize your business.

And guess what . . .

We've all done it the "wrong" way before. This isn't an exercise in shame. In many of Bill's early businesses, he thought it was more efficient to just get to the point and make his pitch in the invite to connect. Those connection attempts were an epic fail with about a zero percent response rate.

Why?

Because people like to feel special, not like a cash machine.

Okay, let's look at a few examples of both great invitation requests and then also the less desirable requests.

Not so great:

"Greeting Bill, I'm National Notary Association Certified in the State of Nevada. I have applied with Snapdocs what other companies you recommending ? Thank you in advance for your time.

Kind Regards"

This one actually started out okay with the first message:

"Bill, I just shared an article with you and I'd love to connect and get your feedback. I'm happy to help any connection in any way I can, I think that's how everyone benefits. I look forward to connecting."

But then, before Bill could respond, the connector followed up with this...

"Hello Bill, Just want to stay in touch as we have more money than houses. As a Direct Private Money Lender, we offer up to 100% financing. This does include 100% of the purchase price, 100% of rehab, and even 100% of closing costs - not to exceed 70% of the ARV. This is for non-owner-occupied residential deals, up to 4 units. All loans are for investing purposes only. I want to do whatever I can to help you grow your real estate business. Since 1984 we have never run out of money!!!! Text me at xxx-xxx-xxxx if you want to talk about getting you the 100% financing I mentioned above."

Great:

"Hi Bill! I'm one of your Thrivers and I'd love to connect with you on Linked In as well, thanks! ;)"

Hi Bill, We exchanged texts recently after I wrote to you about how much I'm learning from your Tuesday Titans! Would be great to connect on LI too. Best wishes."

Hi Bill, FYI the last couple of weeks I've switched from listening to talk radio to listening to your TNT YouTube sessions with Carol and Laura (and guests). Thanks for providing these; they are a great refresher for me to refocus on my notary business. I especially appreciate your session on Notaries over 50. I turn 68 Monday and still love the interaction and helping people. I commend you for your hard work to build your businesses!"

Do you see why these are all great?

They're kind.

They're simple connections.

They're relevant and relatable.

And . . . they don't sell anything!

SUPERCHARGER TIP

At no time send an invitation with an offer or sales pitch! You are building a relationship. Always start by being helpful and interested in other people.

Be Personal and Nurture Your Community

Just because you have connected to someone at one point, it doesn't mean you are always on top of their mind or considered a valuable connection. It's your job to nurture your network, and LinkedIn provides **dozens** of ways to help you do that in a friendly, non-pushy manner. How amazing! Here are just a few tips:

- Always add a personal note with your invitations to connect

- Write a recommendation without being asked

- Authentically endorse someone after they helped you or offered advice or just because you were thinking of them

- Send a charming message with a link to an article they are interested in

- Create valuable and helpful content

- Congratulate and @mention someone who achieved something new

- Comment and start a conversation on your friend's post or article

- Send an audio or video message to a new connection

- Just like or share their posts

CHAPTER 12

LINKEDIN GROUPS

You may or may not find value in participating in LinkedIn Groups. The key is to be strategic and smart about your time. Start by understanding groups, and leverage your time and effort for maximum success.

The benefits of being a group member on LinkedIn include:

- Expands your LinkedIn network

- Makes it easier for people to find you

- Find other people of like interests or professions

- Search members within the group by geography or industry or other filters

- Ability to create a post within the group

- Ability to engage with group member content

- Messaging capability

- Invite group members to connect

- Invite connections to join the group

- Ability to meet or e-meet group members or admins

- Display the group on your profile

Group Classifications

LinkedIn Groups are classified as either *listed* or *unlisted*. Listed groups are searchable. Both managers and members can invite or approve member-ship in standard groups. Unlisted groups are not searchable, and member-ship is only available through manager invitation. A majority of your groups will be listed.

Here is an example of a private, unlisted group. This is Sandra's group for the *LinkedIn Personal Best Club*, which is members only. Sandra invites group members or sends them a special link to join.

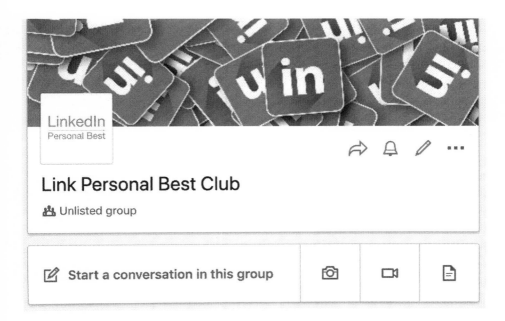

Five Types of LinkedIn Groups to Consider Joining

1. Your university alumni groups. These may be university-managed or independent of your school. Some larger universities have dozens of groups to choose from, sometimes broken out by department, fraternities, and so on.

2. Your organizations. The organizations you belong to probably have LinkedIn Groups and Facebook pages. The group allows you to stay connected in between your monthly meetings. This might be Toastmasters, Chamber of Commerce, or BNI, for example.

3. Community or geographic-based groups. Search for these niche groups that might be valuable for you. This might be city or county specific for you, like "Prescott small business owners," etc.

4. Customer or Prospect groups. Consider where your customers spend their time online. Find your target market in LinkedIn Groups. Think about and research what kind of groups estate planning attorneys, escrow officers, real estate agents, loan officers, etc. might be a part of.

5. Notary association or networking groups. We found 185 groups on LinkedIn with the word *notary*. Below is a sampling of a few you might be interested in joining.

Real Estate, Mortgage, Title & Notary Referral Network
Group • 12,624 members

This is a group that is designed for motivated individuals who are interested in networking in the Real Estate Industry. Use this group as a tool for you to exchange information and opportunities. Real Estat...

Notaries and Notary Signing Agents
Group • 10,742 members

A group of notaries and notary signing agents with focus on networking and business building. All notaries are welcome.

NNA - Notary General Discussion Group
Group • 10,664 members

Notaries of all experience levels are invited to discuss news, issues, resources, Notary best practices and strategies that affect your profession.

NNA - Notary Signing Agents Group
Group • 9,298 members

Notary Signing Agents and mortgage industry professionals are invited to discuss news, issues, resources, Notary best practices and strategies that affect your profession.

NNA - Notary Professionals Group
Group • 4,876 members

Notaries working in specialty fields including Healthcare, Finance, Law, and others are invited discuss news, issues, resources, Notary best practices and strategies that affect your profession.

In addition to national notary groups, you will find LinkedIn groups for notaries in various states such as California, Texas, Massachusetts, and New York.

Evaluate Your Group Options

Now that you have found groups to join, it's time to prioritize the groups as they relate to your brand, goals, and network. Here are some questions to ask about each group you are considering.

- How many members are in the group?

- Who is the owner or admin of the group? Is this someone I should connect with?

- Who belongs to this group? What professions do they represent?

- Are the conversations helpful and high quality?

- What are the group rules?

- Do the member posts uplift, inspire, or inform?

- Are they kind to each other and others outside the group?

Post Content to Groups

You can post your content—or third-party content—into a group. In advance, look for the group rules as they pertain to content and follow them! Veering from the rules may put you into a more restricted status with all LinkedIn Groups and managers.

Here is generally good advice for any group: Don't post advertisements or information about your product or service. Don't post links unless the group allows it. Many groups with an overload of links and ads become very spammy. Instead, post helpful thought leadership questions and comments.

LinkedIn Groups can help you be found on a search, find or hire someone, be noticed for your expertise, and build a network. LinkedIn Groups are part of the thought leadership opportunities available on LinkedIn.

Before we move on to the content section, let's define *thought leadership*. You can absolutely become a thought leader by creating and sharing content on LinkedIn and other platforms, so let's take a look at this.

According to Denise Brosseau, the CEO of The Thought Leadership Lab, we can define thought leaders as "informed opinion leaders and the go-to people in their field of expertise. They are trusted sources who move and inspire people with innovative ideas, turn ideas into reality, and know and show how to replicate their success. Over time, they create a dedicated group of friends, fans and followers to help them replicate and scale their ideas into sustainable change not just in one company but in an industry, niche or across an entire ecosystem."

Wikipedia offers a more simplified definition that summarizes the role: "A thought leader is an individual or firm that is recognized as an authority in a specialized field and whose expertise is sought and often rewarded."

As you share your own journey, create compelling, informative, and in-spiring content, start commenting and contributing on the content of oth-ers, and grow your own expertise through experience, you, my friend, are a thought leader and influencer.

CHAPTER 13

LINKEDIN CONTENT INTRO

LinkedIn content leads to real conversations and genuine opportunities—nearly every day of the year. Bill and Sandra know this from first-hand experience!

Content leads to conversations, which in turn lead to collaborations, sales, interviews, and partnering. CEB (now part of Gartner) says that the average buyer spends 57% of their time online navigating their purchasing journeys before ever speaking to a seller. What are they doing instead? Researching, reviewing profiles, reading articles and posts, checking websites, scouring company pages, and seeking advice from their network. Your content and engagement will position you well and early on.

Hold up. What's on your mind after reading that last paragraph? Does it sound anything like, "Yadda, yadda, Sandra and Bill. Who cares if the average buyer spends 57% of their time navigating their purchasing journey online? I am not in sales; I am a Notary!"

We invite you to explore the idea that no matter what business (or employment) you're in, you *are* in sales. You may actually be selling a product or service, or you may be selling your expertise, your personality, or your life-style.

As a mobile notary and loan signing agent, you do have a service you provide, so you have to find customers to actually use that service. That is sales. Sales are the lifeblood of *any* business, because without clients or customers, (i.e. sales!) you don't even have a business.

SUPERCHARGER TIP

Your LinkedIn content becomes a valuable part of your body of work. Your posts, articles, and videos reflect your brand and attract people to you.

Types of LinkedIn Content

There are multiple content choices on LinkedIn, and they all have unique characteristics.

Posts or status updates	Posts appear in the home feed or might be *Featured*. Posts may be straight text posts or include images, links, documents, or videos.
Native video	Upload from a mobile phone or laptop. The videos will display as a post on the home feed and may now be *Featured*. Learn more in Chapter 15.
Live video	Do a live show on LinkedIn from your personal or company page. Learn more in Chapter 15.
Document posts	Upload a PDF or PowerPoint as part of a LinkedIn post for the home feed or add them to their own *Featured* section. Learn more in Chapter 15.
Polls	Increase engagement and conversation by asking constructive questions with LinkedIn's polling feature. Learn more in Chapter 15.
Stories	Stir your creative juices by creating a short, powerful piece of content. See Chapter 15.
Special Posts	Consider such options as *Find an expert, Celebrate an occasion, Give kudos,* or *Now hiring*.
Articles	Use the article feature for long-form blog content. Articles and long-form blogs appear on your profile and may also be *Featured*. Learn more in Chapter 16.

SUPERCHARGER TIP
Content features are free on LinkedIn!

Where can I post?

LinkedIn posts in the home feed have become the gold standard for LinkedIn content. LinkedIn posts or status updates allow us the opportunity to meet new people, attract interest, gain visibility, and build relationships.

There are three places to produce a post or status update on LinkedIn:

• Home feed (personal profile)

• Group feed

• Page feed (company)

Try the Mobile App for Post Creation and Engagement

The LinkedIn Mobile app is an easy way to actively post, comment, or like in the home feed. With it, you can upload images and videos directly from your phone.

Example Text Post

Look at Sandra's post below, including the emojis and hashtags. As you'll see, she tries to engage her community with a question.

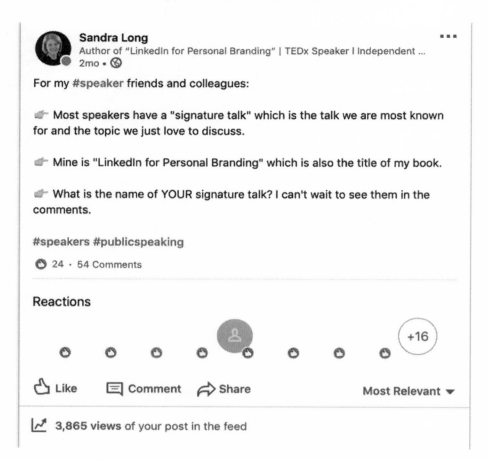

Sandra Long
Author of "LinkedIn for Personal Branding" | TEDx Speaker | Independent ...
2mo • 🌐

For my #speaker friends and colleagues:

👉 Most speakers have a "signature talk" which is the talk we are most known for and the topic we just love to discuss.

👉 Mine is "LinkedIn for Personal Branding" which is also the title of my book.

👉 What is the name of YOUR signature talk? I can't wait to see them in the comments.

#speakers #publicspeaking

⊙ 24 · 54 Comments

Reactions

👍 Like   💬 Comment   ↪ Share   Most Relevant ▼

📈 **3,865 views** of your post in the feed

Example Link Post

Here is Bill's link post. This is an invitation to listen to a show.

 Bill Soroka • 1st   • • •
Author, Sign & Thrive: How to Make Six Figures as a Mobile Notary and Lo...
1w • 🌐

Does your state allow you to communicate with signers using a translator?
Chances are, they do not, except for one state. Tune in to TNT this week to hear
more about that. - https://bit.ly/2M4v4wu

Activity Section – now view content on the profile!

Are you active with the content on LinkedIn? Many people will come to your profile and then head straight over to view your *content activity section*. What does your LinkedIn activity say about you?

Your personal activity section includes all your LinkedIn activity and is displayed prominently towards the top of your profile. Click over and check out the full activity page for yourself or others. The *All Activity* tab will highlight all your interactions, including likes, comments, and shares. The posts, articles, and document tabs display your own content.

Here is Bill's recent activity page:

From here, you can click over to see his posts, articles, documents, and all activity.

Activity   See all
2,157 followers

 Do you have an understanding of the Lifetime Value of your customers? Don...
Bill shared this
8 Reactions

 There is some upcoming legislation in California that has the potential t...
Bill shared this
3 Reactions

 If you truly believe you're the best notary for the job, and you'll deliver th...
Bill shared this
6 Reactions

 What's the deal with all the backdating requests? As a mobile...
Bill shared this
4 Reactions

Engage with Other People's Content!

You can be visible and energize your network by liking and commenting on what THEY post. Commenting with insights is extraordinarily powerful. Share an industry article along with your exclusive insights on the topic. As an intro to the item you are sharing, be sure to add a comment with a richer meaning or idea about the subject.

SUPERCHARGER TIP

Commenting on other people's posts enhances your visibility and relationships!

Never underestimate the value of commenting! If Sandra and Bill could do only ONE thing relative to content, it would be to comment daily with meaningful, insightful, or supportive notes.

Commenting Tips

- Write longer and insightful comments

- Consider adding emojis or bullet points to enhance the visual appeal

- Be sure to comment back with a @mention (tag)

- Avoid links unless necessary

- Avoid hijacking a post or pushing your own sales agenda

- Congratulate friends and associates

Example comment from Sandra

Sandra Long • You   2h ...
LinkedIn Webinar Speaker | Author of "LinkedIn for Personal Brandin...

The students and staff are so fortunate to have Kathleen Lindenmayer leading the way for career success - everything she does is amazing

The 80/20 Rule for Content Engagement

We recommend that you devote a minimum of 80% of your content activity time to engage with other people on THEIR content, be helpful to your community, provide thought leadership, and share useful insights. Avoid selling or asking for a meeting, or worse—a job or sale. This helpful content strategy will help you build relationships. When you actively share valuable insights and comments, you gain both visibility and credibility.

Then, the other 20% of your content activity should be devoted to creating your own valuable & relevant content to share with your network. Are you ready to dive deeper into content ideas? Let's go!

CHAPTER 14

CONTENT IDEAS AND TIPS FOR NOTARIES

Do content ideas come easily to you? Or do you sometimes just sit and stare at the screen because your mind goes blank when you have to create content, like blogs, posts, and videos?

Hopefully, this chapter will give you some content ideas and tips.

10 Ways to Uncover Topics

Content ideas are everywhere—even when you feel stuck. Some helpful tips:

- Always consider your ideal prospects and think of ideas that might be of help to them

- Ask your customers what they care most about

- Review content already published on LinkedIn (see list below)

- Write congratulatory content to help lift up other people

- Refer to Quora or Reddit to see what questions people are asking about notary work

- Look at notary industry news and share your opinions or insights on what you've read

- Discuss trending news reports that are relevant to the notary industry

- Discuss the latest industry statistics

- Create a word cloud or infographic related to notary industry research

- Share some of the best Twitter or Facebook conversations you come across

- Subscribe to *Google Alerts* to get new ideas about topics and news

SUPERCHARGER TIP

Create content that makes your clients, friends, or partners look great and @mention them!

Content to Avoid or Reconsider

Stay away from promotional or boastful content. Instead, put your expertise and willingness to help front and center. That will draw people to you naturally. Can you occasionally post about one of your own noted accomplishments? Yes, of course—but do so gracefully and surround it with gratitude or a learning perspective.

We also recommend staying away from personal content common on some other social media platform sites (i.e., Facebook). Avoid talking about your family, pets, meals, vacations, favorite politicians, religion, health, or personal and family problems. However, it's fine to occasionally weave in a story or personal reflection as long as it can be done in a professional or business context. Of course, you always need to decide for yourself where to draw the line between the very personal and the businesslike personal.

Make your content a combination of personal and professional. Sandra wrote about a new LinkedIn feature and incorporated it into her personal story. See below:

Sandra Long
LinkedIn Webinars | Author of "LinkedIn for Personal Branding" | TEDx Sp...
1w • 🌐

Is your name hard to 🎤 pronounce ? I can relate to this because my original last name (maiden) was Gustafson. I had to spell and pronounce it for people all the time. My name was common in Sweden, but most of my fellow Americans had trouble pronouncing it.

Now LinkedIn is rolling out an audio feature on your profile so that people can hear exactly how you pronounce your name!
If you are interested, check your mobile 📱 app to see if you have the feature yet.

Do you plan to use this feature? Will you use it for yourself or to learn how to pronounce other people's names?

#pronounce #LinkedIn #feature

🔵 🔵 60 · 36 Comments

Reactions

        +52

 Like   💬 Comment   ➡ Share   Most Relevant ▼

 **4,742 views** of your post in the feed

Client and Prospect Oriented Content

According to LinkedIn, 65% of business prospects agree that vendor content has a significant impact on their purchasing decisions. LinkedIn content is ideal for helping you attract the right prospect or buyer persona.

Consider creating or curating content that:

- Addresses pain points or answers frequently asked questions from prospects or current clients

- Provides your unique perspective on a typical customer's standard problems or issues

- Educates your connections with a helpful step-by-step tutorial, detailed graphic, or handy checklist

- Helps prospects make a mindset shift by overcoming a limiting belief

- Discusses industry trends, opportunities, or issues

- Shares lessons learned

Possible Content Ideas for Notaries:

- Offer a brief lesson on valid ID's in your state (or discuss recent changes like the REAL ID rules for your state)

- Offer suggestions, data, or resources for estate planning (awesome opportunity to share your network of attorneys and more)

- Offer positive reviews of local businesses, based on your personal experience

- The difference between an expert notary and one who does not take the role seriously

The options are endless! And we have curated a list of 52 topics that you can download on this Reader's Resource Website.

Resource Website Reminder:

www.NotaryCoach.com/linkedin

Lots of free resources including 52 Topics just for notaries to use in social media and email content marketing.

Write Content That Highlights Others and Builds Relationships

 Bill Soroka • 1st
Author, Sign & Thrive: How to Make Six Figures as a Mobile Notary and Lo...
6d • 🌐

Did you know that Laura Biewer offers private, one on one coaching for loan signing agents? For nearly two hours, Laura will guide you through the confirmation process, over 30 critical loan documents, how to wrap up, and what to expect with shipping and finalizing your order. She gave away one of these incredible sessions at TNT this week. If you'd like your own, book it now at https://bit.ly/324gvkE and purchase the "Mock Loan Signing" option.

Tuesday Notary Titans

Bill Soroka
Carol Ray
Laura Biewer

Write content that helps your ideal client

Bill Soroka • 1st
Author, Sign & Thrive: How to Make Six Figures as a Mobile Notary and Lo...
1w • 🚫

As a mobile notary and loan signing agent, you're often given directions and
"approval" to do things that might actually be against your state laws. Listen in
this week as the Titans discuss your responsibility to know the difference, and
how to handle it. - https://bit.ly/2M4v4wu

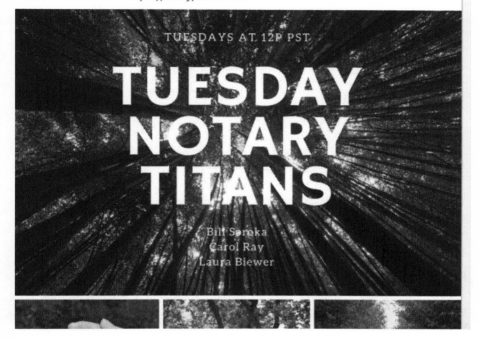

Engaging: Where to Find LinkedIn Content

LinkedIn is a perfect place to start your content engagement journey! It's a platform on which you can find content to curate, share, like, or comment upon. Here's a starting point:

- LinkedIn's search fields (content)

- Your notifications

- Your personal saved hashtags (your hashtag communities)

- Hashtags you select in the search field

- Individual activity pages of prospects, friends, or industry partners

- LinkedIn news feed (currently called LinkedIn Today's News and Views)

- Client, prospect, or partner company page feed

- Feeds from LinkedIn Groups

SUPERCHARGER TIP

Save your hashtags on your account dashboard so you can quickly access your preferred content.

Beyond LinkedIn Content: Finding 3rd Party Content to Share

You may be asking, "How do I find 3rd party content to share or engage with?" The answer is simple—content is available everywhere. First, consider where you already spend time reading and learning. Most articles now provide buttons that easily enable you to share them as LinkedIn posts. You can find content on websites, blogs, industry publications, business publications, and other social platforms. You can also seek out content from top thought leaders and share that, as well.

Content Ideas and Tips for Notaries

Here are a few content sources from our industry:

- The National Notary Association

- The American Society of Notaries

- The California League of Independent Notaries

- The American Land Title Association

- Your State's Secretary of State's Office

- Real Estate and Mortgage Influencers

- Financial Planners

- The Notary Coach Blog

- Laura Biewer's Blog

- Carol Ray's Content through Notary2Pro

- EC Head Notary Training Workshops

- Lots of emerging thought leaders right now!

- Daniel C. Lewis's community and training platform at Lewis Notary Training Services

There are links to these on the book resource website. If you haven't accessed that yet, you can do so at www.NotaryCoach.com/linkedin

Other Content Sources

Here are some other places to look for content to share and discuss:

- Set up a Google alert for Notary Public or Loan Signing agent or mortgage interest rates, etc.

- Business or industry association websites

- Industry blogs

- Other social media platforms

- YouTube or Vimeo

- Social media company pages and feeds

- News articles or industry publications

- Personal activity pages or feeds

SUPERCHARGER TIP

Good content leads to conversations. Conversations lead to relationships. Relationships lead to a thriving business and lifestyle!

Get Organized: Content Calendar Success

Most of us have many content ideas around our specialty topic. But are we organized? Consider pre-planning by implementing a content calendar to:

- save time

- align with your goals

- spot any gaps or opportunities

- batch and manage your work

- stay organized

- team alignment

How to organize your content

- Establish your content goals and ideal target audience.

- Determine pain points and opportunities for your target. What do they care about now?

- Create a repository for all your ideas. It might be a Word or a Google document or a physical file.

- Identify your current content assets (like your blog, vlog, books, etc). Can they be repurposed or reissued?

- Is it valuable over the long term (evergreen) or just temporarily?

- Plan your content for the next month (or longer). Put the creation and promotion time in your calendar to cement your time commitment.

Content Creation Tips for You

Be Yourself

Your LinkedIn connections will respond best if you use your natural voice as you write. Does your content sound authentic to you, and does it sound as if you are speaking? Does your personality shine through? Have you incorporated a story or personal interest? Will your reader learn about you and your perspective? Remember, your goal is to start a conversation with your post, article, or video, so being YOU is essential.

Consider Timing

It is not necessary or even advisable to post every hour or every day on LinkedIn. Many experts insist that spreading out your post frequency will produce better engagement outcomes. Focus on quality first.

In our opinion, the best posting days are Monday through Thursday, but it is also true that there are people online at all days and times of the week. We've noticed that people who engage on Saturdays and Sundays do so almost every weekend. So, if you see that your top prospect is active on Saturdays, become equally engaged with that prospect on Saturdays, as well.

The first hour after your post is magic time on LinkedIn. Use that time for organic promotion and sharing to optimize the impact of that first golden hour.

SUPERCHARGER TIP
Send relevant content directly and privately to your prospects via LinkedIn messaging along with a friendly, helpful note.

Leverage Hashtags

Add up to three hashtags on your LinkedIn posts, articles, or videos. Over-doing hashtags will be viewed as spam by LinkedIn (which makes it different from Instagram). Consider using popular and relevant hashtags so others can easily find your content.

As you select hashtags, consider the number of followers for each one. A slight tweak of wording can make a huge difference. Compare first, so you achieve the best impact.

In addition to industry or topic hashtags, consider a location or event hashtag. Every event today will typically have a unique event hashtag, so you want to leverage that for excellent visibility. You may also want to create and use a company hashtag.

Your hashtags can appear within the copy or at the end of the piece.

Consider these hashtags

#notarynearme

#notary

#notarypublic

#remotenotary

#onlinenotary

#loansigningagent

#yourcity

#mobilenotary

#notarysigningagent

Consider @mentions

Mention others sparingly and carefully. Not everyone likes the mention feature, so try to gauge this before doing so with each person. Creating a post with dozens of mentions looks desperate, and LinkedIn may penalize you if people do not respond. Mention someone when it makes them look great! Almost everyone loves that kind of mention.

Appearance Matters for Content

Posts and articles that have a clean and exciting look should perform better. If your post consists of one long, run-on paragraph, it is doubtful that anyone will want to read it. White space will make it more appealing.

Since you cannot use italics or bold lettering on LinkedIn posts, consider emojis, bullets, and capital letters for a heading. Numbered lists, emojis, or bullets enhance appearance significantly.

For LinkedIn articles, use several images throughout the blog, along with white space.

15 Ways to Promote Your LinkedIn Content Organically

- Send relevant content to a 1st level connection via LinkedIn messaging with a note

- Send it out on Twitter as you post and again afterward

- Post it to Facebook or other social channels

- Add content to the "Featured" section of your profile

- Notify your employees and partners

- Send an email directly to a few people who may be interested in the content

- Actively engage with content from other people, and they are likely to act in kind

- Feature it on your website

- Create adjacent or similar material that points to your post, video, or article

- Focus on promotion within the first hour of posting

- Cross-post into a LinkedIn group (if allowed and appropriate)

- Send a link to an article with a helpful note to people after you connect with them

- Cross-post to your company page feed

- Mention your post in your email newsletter and provide a link

- Cross-post into a Facebook group (if allowed and appropriate)

Repurpose and Reuse Your LinkedIn Content

Yes, it is perfectly permissible to repurpose and reuse content on LinkedIn. But please note that it's best to change up the format, headline, image, or type of content as you do this. For example, you can write a long-form article and then a shortened version as a post. Or write a post or article, create a PowerPoint document on a similar topic, then point one to the other.

SUPERCHARGER TIP
Actively engage and comment on other people's posts to build relationships and increase visibility.

7 Content Tools and Resources

There are many content tools now available. On our book resource website, you can find tools and resources to help you:

- Create your own graphics

- Hire a graphic designer

- Check and fix your grammar

- Create word clouds

- Find and leverage keywords

- Find free images

- Select the best headline for an article

Novice?

Are you concerned about getting started? If you are new to content, start with baby steps. Begin by reading and commenting on LinkedIn first. Get your feet wet while you engage with your network. Engage first and thoughtfully. Become known for inspirational or supportive commenting. When you are ready, you will know it's time to start creating your own posts! As you do so, remember these three categories for content and you can't go wrong:

- Information

- Inspiration

- Sharing your journey and your passion

CHAPTER 15

VIDEOS, POLLS, STORIES, AND MORE

Do you enjoy videos? Well, most of us certainly do. Many of our prospects would rather watch a video than read a post or article. There are different types of videos on LinkedIn, including embedded (3rd party), native, and live.

Embedded Videos (Third Party or Link Videos)

There is a lot of excellent quality content on platforms such as YouTube and Vimeo. LinkedIn provides a fabulous opportunity to cross-promote your top video content. Typically, the view count for LinkedIn is not as high for 3rd party embedded video as it is for the native variety. One reason may be that LinkedIn prefers you to stay on its platform. Sandra and Bill both have embedded videos in their profiles.

What is Native Video?

Native video is a video uploaded directly into LinkedIn from your laptop or phone. The post contains no links to external platforms such as YouTube or

Vimeo. A majority of native video is uploaded directly from smartphones. It's easy and quick. Plus, there are tools you can now use to edit or add captions easily.

Native video will play automatically in the feed, but the viewer needs to turn on the sound. This feature makes sense because many LinkedIn members are at work, so they need control of the volume. We recommend adding captions so people can immediately get a clear understanding of your topic as they scroll on the feed.

Examples of Native Video

Here are a few examples of possible native LinkedIn videos for a notary:

- A 90-second snippet of you sharing an insight for clients
- Short explainer video showing how to navigate a notary situation

Any of those 52 topics we mentioned earlier can be used for quick native videos. You can still download those on this Reader's Resource Website!

Sandra likes to do gratitude videos. This image is a screenshot of her video on LinkedIn. The one minute video below was shared to thank the audience at a conference where she spoke. We can all do a gratitude video or post!

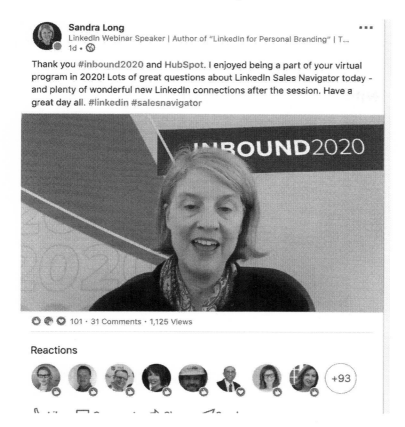

Sandra Long
LinkedIn Webinar Speaker | Author of "LinkedIn for Personal Branding" | T...
1d • ⊚

Thank you #inbound2020 and HubSpot. I enjoyed being a part of your virtual program in 2020! Lots of great questions about LinkedIn Sales Navigator today - and plenty of wonderful new LinkedIn connections after the session. Have a great day all. #linkedin #salesnavigator

○ ◉ ○ 101 • 31 Comments • 1,125 Views

Reactions

+93

Live Video

LinkedIn Live just came onto the scene with some big-time excitement to go along with it. Livestreaming is popular on YouTube, Facebook, and now LinkedIn. Selected LinkedIn users can now host a live show from their profile or company's page. Imagine the opportunities to create real-time interaction with a professional audience! LinkedIn Live allows us to create memorable moments and deepen relationships on the platform easily. Consider streaming from a live event or creating a series. You will need to apply for the feature and then use a 3rd party streaming service to create and post your show.

Bill's YouTube Videos

Check out Bill's profile, and you will find several YouTube videos on his profile. Find one under the experience section and several under the *Featured* feature. He has an active YouTube audience so it's great to link the two platforms in whatever way possible.

Video Content Ideas for Notaries

- A day in the life of a notary
- Insider coverage of industry event or meeting
- Company news
- Industry breakthroughs (news, events, people)
- Industry trends
- The benefits of volunteering or doing good social deeds
- Interviews
- Notary insights
- Storytelling
- Book or podcast reviews
- Introduce team
- Answer common questions often asked by prospects
- How to solve a problem or identify an opportunity
- Motivational
- Values or mission
- Introduce partner
- Explainer videos
- Case studies

Overly personal, controversial, emotional, or loud videos grab attention but don't usually result in a new business relationship. Still, it's a judgment call, so you need to decide your threshold for that type of content.

Making Quality Videos for LinkedIn

Times have changed. You don't need to have a professionally produced video for LinkedIn. However, there are things you can do to create excellent video content for the platform. Here are some tips:

Who	Consider your ideal notary client. Speak to them. Address their concerns. Answer a common question.
What	Make your content valuable and actionable for your prospects.
How	Native or Live? Have good lighting and audio: leverage descriptions, hashtags, and call-to-actions. Make or use an appealing background visual. Consider adding captioning and headings. Be aware of whether your phone should be vertical or horizontal. Each platform can be different.
Timing	Keep it short. The native video needs to be under 10 minutes but is best in the 1-2 minute range to hold onto viewer attention. Live video shows can be longer.
Hook	Start with a compelling opening, no matter what type of video content.
Helpful	Try to be helpful, responsive, and interactive. Be conversational.
Promote	Consider creating a series or a regular cadence to gain follower traction. Announce your live sessions in advance. Cross-promote your videos on email, Facebook, and elsewhere.

Final Tips!	Be authentic.
	Be consistent.
	Test everything first!

LinkedIn Polls

Use this fantastic new poll opportunity to ask relevant questions that your network will WANT to answer. For the most leverage, a poll should be compelling to the reader and also tie into your personal brand, voice, and expertise. For topics, consider asking opinions about:

- How new notary trends impact your clients

- Ask for insights relative to important notary news

- Notary related predictions for the future

- Notary events or programs

- Possible solutions to a business or notary problem

- Take polls for your strategic network (for estate planning, refinances, when they plan to move, etc.)

You can create polls in the home feed, company feed, or in a group. There can be up to four selectable answers for each question. You can also allow comments on your polls. As for the requested timing of responses, you may select one day, three days, one week, or two weeks.

Let's say you are not the poll creator, but merely engaging with someone else's polls. What do you need to know? Your votes are not visible to your network, so it's brilliant to vote AND add your comment for greater visibility and engagement. Keep in mind that the poll author will see your specific answer.

Document Posts

We love this new content option. Now you can share documents, reports, slides, and PDFs on your home feed. This new option allows you to share more of your work than ever before.

Make your documents visually appealing and apply the same content best practices, such as @mentions and hashtags. For PowerPoint, a 5 to 10-page deck works best. Be aware that your readers may download your work from the feed, so remember to add your logo throughout and contact information at the end.

Ideas for document posts:

- White paper
- Presentation
- E-Book
- Case study
- Insights or trends report
- Research study
- How-to guide
- Excerpt from course lecture

Sandra's Document Post Example

During the COVID-19 pandemic in early 2020, Sandra created this PDF slide document on how to warm up your network using LinkedIn. She prepared this document as a resource because people still needed to connect and keep up with relationships, even if it was exclusively online.

 Author of "LinkedIn for Personal Branding" | TEDx Speaker | LinkedIn | So...
2mo • Edited • ⊗

Working from home? Wondering how to keep your sales and career networking going without being over the top? The fact is that your prospects are home working on their laptops too. What can you do?

Use LinkedIn to keep things warm in this unusual business climate.

Let me know which of these ideas YOU are doing this week? Or add your own ideas to the list.

#workfromhome #linkedin #workfromanywhere

LinkedIn Stories

While your opinions of the stories you see on Instagram and Facebook may vary wildly, be ready to embrace the stories you view on LinkedIn! They provide a snackable, quick, brief, and often powerful way to impact your LinkedIn tribe regularly.

There are several benefits of LinkedIn Stories, among them:

- Visibility

- Thought leadership

- Branding

- Networking

- Connecting

- Messaging

LinkedIn Stories are available for personal home feeds and company pages. You may upload an image or a video that is under 20 seconds in duration. They only last for 24 hours, so you want to be able to produce them quickly. Find all the current specs and particulars about LinkedIn Stories in our Reader Resources website.

Story Ideas for Notaries

You will find many ways to get creative with LinkedIn Stories. Here are a few ideas to get you started:

- Quick tips

- A small snippet from your speech

- Case studies

- Notary insight

- Event updates or news (before, during, and after)

- Newsflashes and how they connect to your clients

- Answers to popular notary questions

- Motivational or inspirational commentaries

- Behind the scenes secrets and previews

- Holiday greeting

Consider all the content options on LinkedIn.

To summarize, LinkedIn's video, document, polls, and story options are rapidly transforming our content opportunities on this fantastic platform. LinkedIn is constantly changing and adapting all of its content options. Always consider how you wish to share your thought leadership. Remember that today's buyers, prospects, employers, and candidates will develop an impression of you based on your LinkedIn content. Enjoy the journey!

CHAPTER 16

LINKEDIN ARTICLES

LinkedIn articles are an excellent way to share your body of work and have it available on your profile permanently and over time for your connections, prospects, and clients. Your article can attract and impress people.

Consider your content goals before deciding to post a short-form update or a long-form article. If your content is shorter in length and time-based, the regular short-form post (which we discussed in earlier chapters) is usually best. If you write content that has long term relevancy and is lengthy, consider writing a LinkedIn Article.

Benefits of Posting Articles on LinkedIn's Publisher Platform

Blogging on LinkedIn offers everyone the chance to become a writer. If you are a subject matter expert, then why not show your thought leadership by blogging?

Five Benefits of Blogging on LinkedIn

1. Enhance your thought leadership brand. Writing on LinkedIn builds your brand as a thought leader. The topics you select are a direct tie to you and your work. LinkedIn Articles provides you the opportunity to create and display a portfolio or body of work. Articles become your long-term evergreen brand asset. And now, you can highlight them on the *Featured* section of your profile.

2. Expand your visibility. As your friends and colleagues like and comment on your article, your more extensive second and third-level connected network will become exposed to you and your content. Repurpose and repost your articles for greater visibility. Google may also index LinkedIn blog posts for long term external visibility.

3. Engage and network. Send your work to relevant people who may be interested to learn more. You may also receive direct messages from your readers. Consider featuring other people in your writing and possibly @ mentioning them, which builds relationships and engagement. As a result of publishing, expect to receive new invitations, connections, and followers.

4. Generate leads. Your prospects may subtly self-identify with comments or direct messages after reading your article. Or they may message you after reading your articles and profile. Add a call-to-action at the end of your article to generate leads from interested parties.

5. Platform power and ease. The LinkedIn publishing tool is easy to use and affordable. It's completely free! You will also benefit from the opportunity to include images and other content, the article analytics, and the ability to share inside and outside of LinkedIn very easily.

LinkedIn articles are a valuable content tool for thought leaders. Even if you are not quite ready to start blogging, start by finding and engaging with articles written by others. Consider responding to, liking, and commenting on the articles written by your network associates.

Case Study: Here is the image and headline for Lorraine Schechter's Article

An Introduction to Reverse Mortgages

Published on September 1, 2020

Lorraine Schechter
Mobile Notary Public | Serving Individuals and Businesses | Certified Loan
Signing Agent | Trust Signing Agent | Certified Reverse Mortgage Signing...
1 article ✓ Following

Ten Tips on How to Use LinkedIn Articles

The LinkedIn blogging platform is straightforward to use and navigate. Here are ten tips on making the most of the LinkedIn Publisher platform:

1. Write valuable blog content. The best way to use LinkedIn Publisher is to post a helpful long-form evergreen article. Don't make the mistake of publishing an advertisement, announcement, or link-centric post. Instead, consider writing a Top 10 list, how-to guide, top tips, strategy piece, values post, industry trends, or a compilation type of article.

2. Write longer articles. The minimum length should be 500 words but always shoot for 1,500 to 3,000 words if possible. Many reputable studies have suggested that longer posts are shared more often.

3. Select the right headline for your post. Here are three great reasons: your potential readers will immediately notice your headline, so you want to make it enticing to read and like. Your headline and image are viewable on your LinkedIn personal profile.

4. Incorporate great images. Add a header image that pops and ties into your blog post. Also, consider adding multiple images within the article.

5. Go multi-media. Add relevant slides, video, code snippets, and hyper-links. You can make a corresponding SlideShare presentation or video for your articles. You may wish to link over from the LinkedIn Publisher platform to SlideShare or YouTube.

6. Use shorter paragraphs and heading tags. Make your content easy to read and visibly attractive with white space. Many people today prefer bite-size chunks of information. Take advantage of the H1 and H2 tags for your headings.

7. End your article with a call to action of some kind. Ask a question or ask for comments on your content. Ask for follows, connections, tweets, feedback, PDF downloads, or to book a call with you.

8. Promote. Share your post outside of LinkedIn. Share on Facebook, Twitter, Pinterest, and all of your social media channels. Within LinkedIn, consider which groups to share the article with, being mindful of group rules and culture. Repurpose your articles for higher long-term value. Come back at a future date and recirculate your article again. Add a "click to tweet" option to promote via Twitter easily.

9. Respond to comments, shares, and likes. Send a thank you InMail or message to your connections for greater visibility. Publicly thank the people who comment. This step is crucial for your success, so don't overlook it!

10. Analyze and improve. LinkedIn will display information about article views, reactions, reshares, and reader demographics. Use this information to improve and fine-tune your writing. Use the analytics as well as the comments and feedback to refine your article or future articles. You may also edit a LinkedIn article at any time.

Here's an example of one of Bill's articles, which is geared to notaries.

Public Speaking For The Notary Public

Published on July 5, 2019

Bill Soroka

Create a Newsletter!

Do you have expertise around a topic that will spawn lots of content opportunities? Consider creating a newsletter and publishing articles to your subscribers regularly! Newsletter writing is a fantastic way to get visibility and build brand credibility.

The benefit of newsletters is getting subscribers who are notified of your article publication!

Newsletter Tips:

- Pick a compelling name that clearly articulates the content of the series.

- Create and upload a logo for your newsletter.

- Create or source a captivating cover image for each article in the series.

- Select a compelling headline for each article in the series.

- Establish a schedule or regular cadence for publishing, so your readers are activated.

- Aim for engagement by asking a question at the end of your piece.

- Add a bio with links at the very bottom after a separator line. Ask your readers to subscribe or add another CTA (Call to Action).

- Increase your reach. Share your newsletter articles or page to your network via Facebook, Instagram, Twitter, LinkedIn, and email. Encourage your website visitors to subscribe.

Publishing on LinkedIn can be professionally rewarding and gratifying! Why not start today?

CHAPTER 17

AVOID BILL'S MISTAKES

Bill here. I am going to start writing in first person for the next couple of chapters because I want to share *exactly* how I used LinkedIn to cultivate the relationships that changed everything in my business.

I also just want to drive home the incredible opportunity you have to avoid making the same mistakes I and thousands of notaries before me made in trying to build this relationship-based business.

I've had an Escrow Officer tell me my LinkedIn profile "sucked," and she wouldn't do business with me. Back then, I barely remembered I even had a LinkedIn profile, much less kept it updated and optimized. I was so embarrassed and so disappointed in myself.

What was painfully obvious is that many more Escrow Officers I had reached out to had probably done the same thing she had and researched me on LinkedIn. Not all of them had the nerve, the gall, or the personality type to tell me what they found about me "sucked."

They just faded away . . .

And that's an important lesson to sit with. What your prospects *don't* say to you is almost as important as what they do say to you. When your customers just "fade away" like that, you never know how many relationships, opportunity, and revenue you may have lost. How much did I lose? Dozens of potential clients? Hundreds? In a business where just one single contact can earn you well over $100,000 in revenue every year, that is an insane amount of lost potential.

All because I didn't put in a little time to create the brand reputation I wanted.

If you're going to go through the effort to find, connect, follow-up, and cultivate the customers that are perfect for your business, then you must absolutely do some groundwork ahead of time, so when those prospects do give you a chance, take your call, and then do their own due diligence to make sure you are as quality as you tell them you are, they find the information they need to support that.

That's your LinkedIn profile. That's your LinkedIn content and activity.

So, now that you are sold on how important all that you have learned so far in this book is, and you have implemented that knowledge, how do you use LinkedIn to intentionally grow your business every single day?

Here's how I did that.

Nearly everyone that you may consider an ideal client for your mobile notary and loan signing business will be on LinkedIn in one form or another. In fact, if your ideal customer is an escrow officer, branch manager, or mortgage loan officer for a major corporation, they may actually be required to have a profile and presence on LinkedIn.

It's just good business for the same reasons for them as it is for you—*their* ideal customers are on LinkedIn too!

Think about that for a minute. Your ideal customers are on LinkedIn, (hopefully) with an optimized profile, putting their best face forward; commenting, liking, and sharing other people's content; and creating their own articles or content, hoping other people (like you) will comment, like, and share it, so more of their ideal customers will see it.

See what a cool cycle this is?

You can learn so much about your prospects just by paying attention to their Activity Log. This is the "inside" information that you can use to create a unique and authentic connection strategy.

In my book *Sign & Thrive: How to Make Six Figures as a Mobile Notary and Loan Signing Agent*, I share my full Morning Mastery system that helped elevate my revenue, my relationships, and my peace of mind by 20 times. I created a mini-course about it, and you can have that for free on the resource website for this book.

Implementing specific habits into my day literally took me from making just $1,000 a month as a loan signing agent to making over $20,000 per month within 90 days. I called these my Daily Do's, and although results cannot be guaranteed, I'd still like to share them here with you. Then, we will look very specifically at which steps LinkedIn will serve you best on.

Some Prerequisites

We can't just dive into the Daily Do's without a little background and prerequisites. I don't want you to think I am this super-disciplined entrepreneur who just rolled out of bed one day and said, "Yeah, A+B=C (20)X," solved the equation of my business, and started making $240k per year.

It wasn't like that . . . at all.

I've failed in business far more than I've succeeded. And I've failed mainly because of my resistance to habits and routines that support my goals and growth. I spent the first half of my life bouncing from idea to idea, one business to another, never really gaining any traction. Sometimes I would have five or six little ventures going at the same time, none related to each other at all, pulling my energy in all kinds of different directions.

I loved working on the fun stuff. I can't tell you how many logos I've designed or how many GoDaddy websites I've built (the drag and drop kind—just pretty pictures and a good layout). But when it came to the activities that truly "moved the needle" on my business, I was lost. Some of it was hard. Some of it was outside my scope of skills, and I needed to learn. Some was doable if I just did it.

But all of it required consistent action. That happened to be my greatest weakness at the time. Apparently, I liked to learn lessons the hard way too, because even with flop after flop, I never changed my behavior.

So, five of the remaining six ventures I had completely collapsed. That sixth business was this little mobile notary and loan signing business that I had the absolute least expectations for. And at that time, I had no idea of the potential it had. I went years "abusing" this business, not giving it the respect it deserved, and I am so glad I pulled my head out of my rear (and just in time).

As I tried to pick up the pieces, broke and nearly destitute, I spent an entire Thanksgiving weekend alone, drowning in tears and vodka, determined to figure out why this kept happening. After 26 attempts at business, why couldn't I make even just ONE work?

I started with a "results inventory." What did I have? What skills, lifestyle, income, possessions, thoughts, mindset was I currently in possession of? And what did I want to have? The difference between those two realities was the gap.

And it was a helluva gap.

I knew I had it in me to be an entrepreneur. If nothing else, I just could NOT go back to another call center job to pay the bills.

I read all the books, went to every seminar and workshop I could afford (and then some), had the enthusiasm and the desire to make this happen, so what gives?

After discovering people like Brendan Burchard, BJ Fogg, and Hal Elrod, I finally realized what was missing, the common denominator—habits and the string of habits known as a routine.

I had resisted them my entire life, thinking that only boring people had habits. I was wrong. The most interesting people, those who have dreamed, achieved, and helped others do the same, all live and breathe by some sort of routine.

I guess when the student is ready the teacher appears, because I had heard all that before but never did anything with it.

Avoid Bill's Mistakes

Over the next few months, I dove into habits, reading, and re-reading Hal Elrod's *The Miracle Morning* and implementing all six of his S.A.V.E.R.S. practices for 90 days. I spent that 90 days completely unexcited about my notary business. In fact, to me it was a dead business, too. I had a couple of clients that fed me enough signings to make about $1,000 a month, but I was looking for the next opportunity.

And even though I didn't have a business I loved yet, my peace of mind was through the roof, and I felt amazing. *The Miracle Morning* kept the depression at bay and allowed me to be present, ready for the next big thing.

That next big thing was a conversation with my friend Jamie, sitting at a bar on a Sunday afternoon. She said, "Billy (that's what my friends call me), why don't you apply all this knowledge you've accrued through 26 failed businesses to this notary business that keeps paying you?"

Well, duh!

Why didn't I think of that?! This was another example of when the student is ready, the teacher will appear. Jamie was my teacher that day, and the light bulb went off, and the flood gates opened.

I was going to make this business work.

Chapter 18

WINNING LINKEDIN EVERY DAY

The Daily Do's

Below is a list of those activities I did on a daily basis to help pull me out of the hole I was in after 26 business failures and start earning more money than I ever had in my life. As you'll see, too, these activities are designed to connect us to people, so a side effect of trying to grow my business was deeper relationships and more peace of mind.

As a hustlin' mobile notary and loan signing agent, you can expect that your phone may start ringin' and dingin' as soon as closing agents and schedulers get into the office around 8:00am. That's good news of course, because working *in* your business and doing the things that earn immediate income is important. But it is *not* everything.

You must spend time working *on* your business too. That's the big picture stuff, like what I'll show you here with the Daily Do's. These are the actions that will get you out in the "arena," meeting the very people that will make opportunity happen for you.

What that meant for me was, I had to learn how to become a "morning person." And it wasn't easy, especially because I often worked as a bartender and a poker host well into the night. You may have similar circumstances or family obligations that stretch you thin. I get it. And, if you want to make this business succeed, you'll find a way. If you want an excuse to fail, you'll find that too.

These Daily Do's were performed as early as 4am on most days. I went a little nuts. I was desperate, and I needed a win. Not just to pay bills. But to know I *could* do it. These are all scalable, so you can slow down or speed up to make these fit into your own vision. Maybe you don't want to work as hard as you have to make $364,000 a year. That's okay! Take what works for you; pitch the rest.

The Daily Do's:

- Add 3-5 names to your contact list daily*
- Ping 10 people from your list*
- Send 1-10 greeting cards
- Stack your meetings and attend a networking event
- Create a separate, "Fab 100" list of people you *want* to work with*
- Research one person from your Fab 100 list*
- Find a creative and unique way to connect*
- Follow up as many times as it takes*
- Ask your network for referrals*
- Write one blog or social media post daily*

How LinkedIn Helps with the Daily Do's

On each of the Daily Do's I have listed out, I added an asterisk to the end of each one that you can use LinkedIn to help complete. Take a look at that real quick. 8 out of the ten Daily Do's can be done with or on LinkedIn. And I would venture to say we could actually find a way for LinkedIn to help with those remaining two as well.

You can see now that there is no question about how valuable LinkedIn can be for growing your business, your lifestyle, your relationships, and, of course, your income. Let's dive in to each one of these eight different 'Do's' and share how I used LinkedIn for them.

SUPERCHARGER TIP
Add 3-5 Names to Your Contact List Every Day

By now, this might seem a bit obvious to you. Your contact list might actually just be your LinkedIn "Connections" list. You might also have a spreadsheet or a CRM too, but what this exercise does is get you talking about your business, talking about other people's business, and laying the foundation for relationships later.

Use the strategies in this book to connect to your ideal prospects or *their* prospects on LinkedIn. This counts as adding names to your contact list!

SUPERCHARGER TIP
Ping 10 People from Your Contact List Every Day

Create a Fab 100 List

Your Fab 100 list is like your wish list of clients. Obviously, you don't have to create this list every single day, but you want it front and center.

For me, I had major homebuilders, title companies I used to drive by every day, and even some of the top performing real estate agents in Arizona on my list. Why real estate agents? Because I know they ALL have *at least* three favorite escrow officers that they LOVE to work with, and I wanted referrals.

LinkedIn is the perfect platform to find the people you most want to work with. First of all, even with the free version of LinkedIn, you can search by company name, title, or industry (even geographically).

Second, you may very well already be connected with the people you want to do business with, so going through your LinkedIn connections can help you fill your Fab 100 list.

Research One Person from Your Fab 100 List Every Day

LinkedIn is a researcher's dream. It is full of your ideal customers sharing their big wins, their dreams, and their own customer's information. Plus, thanks to the About and experience section, you have a chance to get to know your ideal customer a bit, which greatly warms up the contact you're about to make.

What we are looking for here is something you can either congratulate them on, help them with, or relate to. That's it. We are NOT trying to stalk anyone or learn their most intimate secrets. We just want a reason to pop in and say hi.

Ping 10 People from Your List

Pinging is just a gentle nudge to remind your contacts that you exist. It's another way to stay top of mind. Some of the most common ways to do this is to use @mentions on a post, tagging someone, sharing someone's content (they get notified of that, so that's a ping), or sharing content to someone's page.

You can also ping by sending a quick note through the LinkedIn messaging app. Remember, these are already people you are connected with, and you also want to use the strategies from this book when sending a note. We're not selling! We're just checking in, congratulating, encouraging, or just wishing them a great day.

Some of my favorite things to find on a LinkedIn profile:

- Recent promotions

- Breaking sales records

- VIP Club or other company victories, sales clubs, etc.

- New hires

- Moved offices

- Now hiring or recruiting (I like to introduce any friends or acquaintances I have that are looking)

- Sports they play

- Philanthropic endeavors

- Spiritual/Churches they attend

- Universities or College

Do you see any opportunities for connection here? Anything you might be able to help with? See something to give a "high five" for? Can you relate to anything? That's all we're looking for in this step, and LinkedIn is perfect for it.

Find a creative and unique way to connect to that one person each day

Okay, so through your research on LinkedIn, you've just found some info that you can either relate to, help with, or cheer this person on with. Now all you have to do is send it over to them. You have a couple of options. You can use LinkedIn messaging, or you can send through traditional email.

Personally, I've always preferred email because my response rate has been higher . . . or faster, anyway. Choose what is right for you!

Here are a few examples of the kind of messages I am talking about. Also, remember your learning from earlier in the book. We are NOT selling in these messages, and the goal is not to drown our prospects in words about how great we and our services are. We are aiming to help, congratulate, or resonate.

- Recent promotions — *"Hi Marcy! I just saw the news on your promotion to branch manager and I wanted to say congratulations!!! What an exciting time for you to be leading your company in this business. Take care and please let me know if I can support you in any way!"*

- Breaking Sales Records — *"Wow! John, congratulations on breaking another record XYZ Title! You're an inspiration, my friend. Let me know if I can do anything to support you along the way!"*

- VIP Club, or other company victories, sales clubs, etc. — *"Hey Alena, Way to rock it again for VIP Club this year! It seems like just yesterday they were sending you off to Puerto Vallarta to celebrate your last big win. Are they taking a trip this year? Congratulations, and as usual, if I can do anything to support you along the way, don't hesitate!"*

- New hires — *"Hi Samantha, congratulations on your new position with XYZ Title. I am always so impressed with how well they take care of their customers, so I am sure you'll be right at home there. John blows me away too! If I can support you in any way through this transition, please don't hesitate to reach out!"*

- Moved offices — *"Hi Valerie, congratulations on your new office space! It looks absolutely gorgeous! If you have an open house to break it in, I'd love to participate. If you're looking for sponsors, I may even be interested in that too! Just let me know the details. Congrats again!"*

- Now hiring or recruiting (I like to introduce any friends or acquaintances I have that are looking) — *"Hey Jim, I just saw your post looking for the new entry level escrow assistant and I think I have the perfect person for you. His name is Luis Garcia and I'll have him apply as per your instructions in the post. Congrats on your continued growth and success!"*

- Sports they play — *"Hey Jennifer! I just noticed you play softball in the Scottsdale city leagues. I just moved to Old Town and was looking for a team. Do you have any recommendations? Or do you have a contact I could reach out to? Maybe I'll see you on the fields!"*

- Philanthropic endeavors — *"Hi Brenda, Wow! I just happened across your youth leadership camp, 'Yaya Kids Camp,' and I am so touched, moved, and inspired, by the work you do there. I am a lifelong advocate for youth, embracing leadership and empowerment on all levels, and I know it takes a lot to get these programs funded and rolling. Thank you for the work you do securing and empowering our future leaders!"*

- Spiritual/Churches they attend — *"Hi Charles, I just noticed you are a deacon at North Phoenix _____ Church. I attend _____ across town and find myself so inspired by the message. Thanks for your commitment to the congregation!"*

- Universities or College — *"Hi Eileen! It's always great to run into a fellow "Bama graduate. Those were some of my favorite years. Graduated class of '00. Go Crimson Tide!"*

Follow Up as Many Times as It Takes

Listen closely . . .

The fortune is in the follow-up. Depending on what industry statistics you look at, your prospects may not make the decision about whether or not to work with you until somewhere between 7 and 15 points of contact.

Sure, sometimes it happens faster, of course. Some people you just immediately jive with, or you connect at precisely the right time.

Most relationships just take a little bit longer. And frankly, when it comes to "fly by night" companies, notaries abound. There are millions of us in the country, but very few that take this business seriously enough to not just connect once, but up to 15 times, just to grow a relationship.

Here's what's cool though. The follow-up can actually be easier than the initial connection. If you're like me, an introvert that despises cold calling, then you may have really had to build yourself up just to make that initial connection. Now, the fun can begin.

Let the conversation flow organically. If you use the model from the previous lesson, most people will respond to you. They may even ask you questions about you and your business. It's just a normal conversation. Be you—the best version of you.

And sometimes, they don't respond because they don't see it, don't have time, or it is of low priority to them. That has nothing to do with you, so don't judge yourself or them for it. Just stay in touch.

Staying in touch is a lot easier with a customer relationship management tool (CRM) but not necessary on LinkedIn. This is where you could use the pinging strategy we talked about earlier just to continue to @mention, tag, or share information.

Ask Your Network for Referrals

You are likely surrounded by people that want you to succeed in your business. Sometimes, you just have to ask for support.

My favorite people to ask are mortgage loan officers and real estate agents. Why? Because they all have their favorite closing agents to work with. And they usually have three or four escrow officers or closing attorneys they *love* to work with for different reasons!

Below is another example of what this conversation might look like. I use this in my Sign & Thrive book, as well as the Morning Mastery course.

Here's a conversation I had with my friend Shane, a loan officer:

Bill: *"Hey Shane, I see you hustlin' and posting such great work for your clients all the time. I am happy for you-Congratulations!"*

Shane: *"Thanks Bill! Looks like you're killin' it too!"*

Bill: *"Yeah, I am loving this mobile notary gig. It's blowin' up more than I ever thought possible! Speaking of which, I am always looking for great escrow officers to work with. Who is your favorite escrow officer?"*

Shane: *"Oh man, I have three that are AMAZING! Maria at Fidelity, Paul at Pioneer, and Imelda at Mirage."*

Bill: *"THREE favorites!!! I love it! What makes them your favorites?"*

Shane: *"Maria is obsessed with details and has perfect files that close on time with no questions asked. Paul takes great care of my clients and has one of those personalities that they just love. Imelda has been in the business for over 30 years and if I have a wonky file, she gets it done!"*

Bill: *"Oh man, these are exactly the kinds of people I want to work with. Would you mind introducing me via email, or with a meeting?"*

Shane: *"I'll do an email intro right now on all three of them! Hope it works out!"*

This is a dream connection. The key is to get the introduction. Just getting a name, or an email address, or just a business card won't cut it. That still may work; don't get me wrong. But an introduction via email or in person will far surpass.

Write One Blog or Social Media Post Every Day

I recently attended an expensive and intensive mastermind weekend put on by one of my favorite gurus, Ray Edwards. Ray is a guy that makes over a million dollars a year doing what he loves—writing sales copy and teaching influencers, business owners, and service providers how to think bigger and build their dream lives.

As we finished up our workshop, I asked Ray, "What is the single most important piece of advice you would give me or any other small business owner if they wanted to 10X their impact and income?"

He said, *"create more content consistently and use social media to distribute that content so more people can find you."*

That's it.

Earlier in this book, Sandra and I gave you some ideas for content to share. Think like an expert and an influencer. Yes, people care about what you say. They want information, and they want inspiration. You've got that!

Plus, you LOVE what you do, so you can share your passionate journey along the way.

Remember, we've got some resources for you on this Reader's Resource Website too, including the 52 topics download. I've also included the "Daily Do's" checklist for your use!

Now, get out there and crush it!

CHAPTER 19

LINKEDIN GOALS

We wish great success for you all on LinkedIn as you grow your business. Like so much in your business, your LinkedIn strategy is not a passive activity. We don't recommend a "set and forget" approach. Once you are engaging, you will discover the richness of opportunities that unfold for you on LinkedIn.

Your Prime Objective

A profile view means someone is interested in you. Your offline and online activity will dramatically impact the number of views on your profile. If you are actively involved in business or community, your views will reflect that activity. So, if you are going on sales calls, meeting with partners, speaking, networking, teaching, writing, attending closings, or meeting people, you can count on more LinkedIn profile views.

Additionally, your *online* activity has a direct correlation to the number of your profile views. If you are adding connections, posting articles, attending Zoom meetups, making mentions, recommending, endorsing, or commenting on posts, you are more likely to be seen and then your profile viewed. If you are observing other people's profiles, they are likely to come back and look at yours. If you are involved in several groups, making comments, and sharing, your visibility will rise.

Let's make it happen on LinkedIn

Here are our specific suggestions for you. These are your main goals:

1. Have an "All-Star" profile with a high quality and motivation factor. Make sure your profile optimistically and authentically represents your brand in the best possible light. Come back and refresh your profile periodically to stay 100% current.

2. Increase the number of strategic first-level connections. This action should increase each week as you meet new people at loan signings, closings, and networking events. Carefully consider each invitation. Be sure to proactively send invitations to build a strategic network that may refer or mention you.

3. View other people's profiles and show genuine interest, and you will grow your own viewer count.

4. Support and strengthen your network. Build relationships by promoting the significant accomplishments of your first-level connections. Offer congratulations, write recommendations, and endorse liberally!

5. Engage more. Increase the quantity and quality of your messages and comments. Your comments and messages will enhance your visibility and relationship opportunities. Aim to add insightful comments every day. Support your friends and colleagues with @mentions, congratulations, kudos, and comments.

6. Think about creating posts or articles on LinkedIn. Make sure you are posting helpful content that will generate interest from others. It should rarely be self-promoting. Great content will generate more followers. Some of your best opportunities will come to you as a result of you being a helpful notary. Inevitably we get asked, "how many times should I be posting?" The answer is—it depends. It depends on what the rest of your social media and content strategy looks like. If you're just starting out,

begin with something that is so easy for you to do that you will actually do it. One post per week? Fine. One post per month? You're pushing it, but if that's all you can muster right now, do it. And here is what is real— your posts and articles should contain value for your prospect. When your content contains value, there is no reason to limit yourself. There are no rules about posting "too much." Gary Vaynerchuck and Grant Cardone broke all the rules and they're millionaires because of it. In an ideal world, you'll find a rhythm to your content (that would be one blog or article per week) supported by three or four social media posts to help spread the word about that blog or article.

7. Increase the number of recommendations and endorsements. Consider giving them first. Be a valuable partner, employer, and colleague by showing this type of genuine support whenever possible. Consider creating a "Recommend and Endorse" day on your calendar so you regularly and consciously do this activity. Put it on your calendar every Thursday, for example. Bill uses Sundays for activities like this because his phone tends to be more quiet.

8. Create your own Daily Do's. Use Bill's, or totally create your own that will support the vision you have for your business and your lifestyle. The key is to schedule it and do it every single day. When you're in full hustle mode trying to build your dream, remember that dreams don't always get weekends off. If you find that by taking the weekends off from your Daily Do's and habits actually throws you off, and it takes you until Wednesday each week to get back on track, do your Daily Do's on the weekends too. Do that until you get the results you want.

9. Add your company on LinkedIn by creating a Page. Why not get visibility for your business?

10. Stay current on the newest LinkedIn updates and opportunities.

You Can Be the "Preferred Notary" That Everyone Remembers – With Help from LinkedIn!

- be the helpful notary expert

- tell your story in your essay

- be uniquely you

- share a perspective or glimpse of you as a person

- be connected to your community

- support your network

Beginner? Just Start with Baby Steps!

Don't let these ideas overwhelm you. Take one step at a time! We recommend that you do the following:

1. Focus on your profile and personal brand first. Put the content plans out of your head for now, and concentrate on having a compelling personal profile.

2. Make sure you have a fantastic headshot, relevant headline, and motivational About essay.

3. Use the best images and language for your personal brand.

4. Connect with all the people in your professional and personal network.

5. Be friendly and helpful.

Direct Feedback

We are open to your direct feedback. If you have a question, idea, or success story, we may incorporate your thoughts into a future edition or article. Please email us at sandra@postroadconsulting.com or orders@notarycoach.com.

Let's Stay Connected

We hope you will decide to stay connected to us after you finish this book. We would like to hear your thoughts, questions, ideas, and suggestions. Also, feel free to contact us if you need more help with LinkedIn or building your notary business!

Connect with us!

Orders@notarycoach.com and sandra@postroadconsulting.com

Websites:

www.notarycoach.com and www.postroadconsulting.com

Please follow us:

Author's LinkedIn personal profiles:

http://ww.linkedin.com/in/billsoroka

http://www.linkedin.com/in/longsandra

Sandra's LinkedIn company page:

http://www.linkedin.com/company/post-road-consulting

Author's YouTube Channels:

http://www.youtube.com/notarycoach

http://www.youtube.com/postroadconsulting

Author's Facebook Pages:

Notary Coach: http://www.facebook.com/notarycoach

Post Road Consulting: http://www.facebook.com/postroadconsulting

Author's Instagram Profiles:

Instagram: http://www.instagram.com/billsoroka (@billsoroka)

Instagram: http://www.instagram.com/sandraglong (@sandraglong)

Author's Twitter Profiles:

@SandraGLong and @NotaryCoach

Online Reviews: Thank you in advance for helping us!

We will be so grateful for your Amazon, Goodreads, and book retailer reviews. All the readers arrive at this book destination from different perspectives and backgrounds, and we hope that you found nuggets in here to help you with your business or career. Thank you in advance for your online reviews!

Here's to Your Success

We genuinely hope you enjoyed this book and that it has spurred your thinking about yourself. We find LinkedIn to be the best current online platform for your personal and professional branding. You could take the same principles here and apply some of the strategies and thinking to Facebook, Google, and elsewhere on social media.

We wish you the ultimate in new business and career success! Thrive on!

—Bill Soroka and Sandra Long

APPENDIX A

SPECIFICATIONS AND CHARACTER COUNTS

The specifications and counts do change periodically due to LinkedIn platform updates. This is the current information as of fall 2020.

LinkedIn Profile Image Specifications and Character Counts

For images, use PNG or JPG file types.

Profile Photo/Headshot

These may be between 400 × 400 and 7,680 (w) × 4,320 pixels (h). The ideal resolution is 400 × 400 pixels. The maximum file size is 8 megabytes: file type PNG or JPG. If you have trouble uploading your photo, try a different browser.

Background Banner Image

The image should be 1584 (w) x 396 (h) pixels with a 4:1 proportion: file type PNG or JPG.

Character Limits

First name	20
Last name	40
URL	5–30
Headline	220
Address	1,000
Website URL	256
Website anchor text	30
About essay	2,600
Company name	100
Position title in the experience section	100
Education	100
Position/experience description	2,000
Education description	1,000
Recommendation	3,000
Honors and awards	1,000
Project description	2,000
Publication description	2,000
Post	1,300
Article headline	100

Other Specifications/Limitations

Choose up to fifty skills.

Choose up to one hundred groups.

THANK YOU FOR READING!

DON'T FORGET YOUR FREE MATERIAL ON THE *SUPERCHARGE YOUR NOTARY BUSINESS WITH LINKEDIN* BOOK RESOURCE PAGE!

GET FREE ACCESS AT
www.NotaryCoach.com/linkedin

Made in the USA
Monee, IL
23 February 2021